T0294818

LIVING HISTORY

American Association for State and Local History Book Series

About the Series
The American Association for State and Local History Book Series addresses issues critical to the field of state and local history through interpretive, intellectual, scholarly, and educational texts. To submit a proposal or manuscript to the series, please request proposal guidelines from AASLH headquarters: AASLH Editorial Board, 1717 Church St., Nashville, Tennessee 37203. Telephone: (615) 320-3203. Website: www.aaslh.org.

About the Organization
The American Association for State and Local History (AASLH) is a national history membership association headquartered in Nashville, Tennessee. AASLH provides leadership and support for its members who preserve and interpret state and local history in order to make the past more meaningful to all Americans. AASLH members are leaders in preserving, researching, and interpreting traces of the American past to connect the people, thoughts, and events of yesterday with the creative memories and abiding concerns of people, communities, and our nation today. In addition to sponsorship of this book series, AASLH publishes *History News* magazine, a newsletter, technical leaflets and reports, and other materials; confers prizes and awards in recognition of outstanding achievement in the field; supports a broad education program and other activities designed to help members work more effectively; and advocates on behalf of the discipline of history. To join AASLH, go to www.aaslh.org or contact Membership Services, AASLH, 1717 Church St., Nashville, TN 37203.

LIVING HISTORY

Effective Costumed Interpretation and Enactment at Museums and Historic Sites

David B. Allison

ROWMAN & LITTLEFIELD
Lanham • Boulder • New York • London

Published by Rowman & Littlefield
A wholly owned subsidiary of The Rowman & Littlefield Publishing Group, Inc.
4501 Forbes Boulevard, Suite 200, Lanham, Maryland 20706
www.rowman.com

Unit A, Whitacre Mews, 26-34 Stannary Street, London SE11 4AB

British Library Cataloguing in Publication Information Available

Library of Congress Cataloging-in-Publication Data

Names: Allison, David B., author.
Title: Living history : effective costumed interpretation and enactment at museums and historic sites /
   David B. Allison.
Description: Lanham, Maryland : Rowman & Littlefield, 2016. | Series: American Association for
   State and Local History | Includes bibliographical references.
Identifiers: LCCN 2016005949 (print) | LCCN 2016007255 (ebook) | ISBN 9781442263802 (cloth :
   alk. paper) | ISBN 9781442263819 (pbk. : alk. paper) | ISBN 9781442263826 (Electronic)
Subjects: LCSH: Museums—Educational aspects. | Museum theater—Educational aspects. | Histori-
   cal reenactments—United States—Case studies. | Historic sites—Interpretive programs—United
   States—Case studies. | History—Study and teaching—United States—Case studies.
Classification: LCC AM7 .A525 2016 (print) | LCC AM7 (ebook) | DDC 069.07--dc23

∞ ™ The paper used in this publication meets the minimum requirements of
American National Standard for Information Sciences Permanence of Paper for
Printed Library Materials, ANSI/NISO Z39.48-1992.

Printed in the United States of America

CONTENTS

Preface   vii
Acknowledgments   xi

1   Introduction: Using Living History to Connect with Visitors   1
2   Putting Living History in Context   5
3   Making Meaning and Creating Authenticity at Museums   21
4   Examining Successful First-Person Interpretation   41
5   Opening Doors at Conner Prairie   63
6   "They're Trying to Learn for Free!": Playing with Living
    History in Pop Culture   83
7   Conclusion: Using Living History for Stronger Programming
    and Education   95

Appendix: Poems on Memory and the Past   99
Bibliography   101
Index   107
About the Author   109

PREFACE

The gulf between the past and the present is ever expanding. As the years pass, we become estranged from the human stories that animate past events. Disembodied dates tied to the "momentous" societal or political changes slowly leech away our empathy and historical imagination. Living history is one of the best ways to bridge the chasm between the past and the present. When a visitor to a museum talks face-to-face with an interpreter portraying a character from the past, they are able to make more meaningful and rich connections to history than almost any other technique. Human beings are made for relationships and conversation. Exhibits, books, and movies can all be effective ways to spark people's interest in history, but first-person characterizations are more dynamic and powerful than any of these other methods because they start from a place of human connection.

Living History is intended for museum professionals. I will show how living history techniques can be used effectively to connect with audiences in a wide variety of museums. Whether you work at a children's museum, history center, science museum, or anything in between, this book will provide the theoretical background and context for living history paired with tangible examples of successful first-person characterizations in action at museums around the country.

Starting with an overview of how living history gained traction as an interpretive technique, this book will provide an in-depth view of the historiographical debates around the interpretation of the past at Colonial Williamsburg, the Henry Ford Museum, and Conner Prairie. Conner Prairie will serve as the primary example, and the morphing goals of that museum over time will be highlighted in detail. Conner Prairie's history is a helpful case study that will provide a solid backdrop for an exploration of the ways that living history techniques are used in museums today.

There are a number of well-established books about theater in museums as well as a plethora of more traditional "museum studies" books that touch on living history techniques. However, since Jay Anderson's *A Living History Reader: Museums* (1991) and Stacy Roth's *Past into Present: Effective Techniques for First-Person Historical Interpretation* (1998), there have been no serious or systematic examinations of first-person characterizations in museums. Sten Rentzhog's *Open Air Museums: The History and Future of a Visionary Idea* (2007) does explore how living history is used at museums around the world, but because the narrative spans Europe and America, it does not have much depth of focus on American museums that fall outside of the traditional living history museum milieu. Rentzhog does not, for example, explore first-person characterizations at science or children's museums.

The most widely read book that touches on anything approaching first-person characterizations is Tony Horwitz's excellent 1998 book, *Confederates in the Attic*, which devotes large swaths of its narrative to the Civil War reenacting community—which most professionals consider to be a bastardized cousin of true living history. Other books about enactment most typically fall into the aggressively theoretical and erudite categories of scholarship. It is high time to redress this gap in real-life experiences and examples from the front lines of museums and give living history its due.

HOW TO READ THIS BOOK

Authors are often plagued by the illusion that their readers will pore over every word of their book. I harbor no such illusion. If you are most interested in the development of Colonial Williamsburg, the Henry Ford Museum, and, in greater detail, Conner Prairie and how these museums struck upon the idea of communicating to the public using first-person characterizations, then you will want to focus on chapter 2, "Putting Living History in Context," chapter 3, "Making Meaning and Creating Authenticity at Museums," and chapter 5, "Opening Doors at Conner

Prairie." If you crave some meaty and immediately applicable lessons from your fellow museum professionals, then flip over to chapter 4, "Examining Successful First-Person Interpretation." If you are looking for a light-hearted romp through the always fascinating world of pop culture representations of the work that we do, head to chapter 6, "'They're Trying to Learn for Free!': Playing with Living History in Pop Culture." I want to model free choice learning in this book. So go ahead and skip around as your interests lead you. There is no shame in being nonlinear.

No matter where you find yourself in the book, you should continually brush up against three touchstone themes. One of these themes is that living history techniques are still alive and well and can be used to help people make meaningful connections to the past. While costumed first-person characterizations are certainly no longer at the cutting edge of museum practice, the human connections that are formed in the conversations between guests and an interpreter are timelessly effective.

A second theme is that listening to your audience should be the beginning, middle, and end of a well-crafted museum experience. A museum can only become truly effective when it is valued and trusted by all the people it currently serves and—perhaps most importantly—by the people that it does not serve but hopes to serve in the future. Becoming a true partner in a constant cycle of dialogue with the community starts with empathetic listening.

The final theme is that museums should leverage entertainment toward the goal of education. Fun has never been a four-letter word. Museums need to embrace the power of joy, laughter, wonder, and awe as they take their rightful place alongside the most effective leisure time venues in the country. We will never be Disney World, but that doesn't mean that we shouldn't try. The worldview that girds Disney does not hold a candle to the educational and potentially world-changing missions of museums. Imagine if our messages of care for the natural world, the power of curiosity, and the imperatives of social justice for all people went down as easily as the messages of consumerism, middle-class privilege, and American exceptionalism that are so easily swallowed at Disney! Becoming more accessible and enjoyable is a worthy pursuit for museum professionals, and my hope is that this book might spur us toward a more playful and conscientious approach to our work.

ACKNOWLEDGMENTS

Museum professionals are a tight-knit, forthcoming group. We love to celebrate successes and support each other. This book was enhanced greatly by the contributions of a wide range of museum professionals and colleagues from across the country.

Cathryn Ferree, Catherine Hughes, and Ellen Rosenthal were hugely helpful in reconnecting me with the new approaches and innovations that have emerged at Conner Prairie since 2010. Jennifer Holland and Elizabeth Wood at The Children's Museum of Indianapolis made connections for me with the right folks who could share their passion for and expertise with live interpretation in *The Power of Children* exhibit.

Dale Jones from *Making History Connections* provided some great leads early in the project and continues to be an insightful champion of first-person characterization.

Special thanks to Sarah Fischer—who wields a wonderful set of writerly eyes—Michael Parker, Jennifer Moss-Logan, José Zuniga, and the rest of the superb enactor team at the Denver Museum of Nature and Science (DMNS), who all provided helpful and critical feedback on early versions of chapters. Nancy Walsh and Dr. Bridget Coughlin at DMNS have been constant supporters and encouragers throughout this process, and I am deeply indebted to them both for their generosity.

Dr. Nancy Robertson drove much of the scholarship and writing toward the most interesting and impactful stories between 2006 and 2010 as I worked on my thesis (upon which this book is based). For that I remain grateful. Indiana University–Purdue University, Indianapolis's History

Department faculty are strong advocates of new ways to provide access to history for the public and, along with Ken Bubp, shepherded many of my nascent ideas around the importance of intermixing history and audience needs in unique ways.

The folks at the American Association for State and Local History, in particular Bob Beatty, continue to support the efforts of museums in meaningful and varied ways. Rowman and Littlefield's Charles Harmon has been a strong and consistent editor, and I appreciate his input greatly.

My three delightful daughters and, most of all, my amazing wife Molly are the beautiful bedrock of faith, hope, and love for my life, without which this book would not exist. Thank you, my dears.

I

INTRODUCTION

Using Living History to Connect with Visitors

American museums stand at the nexus of civic religion, community engagement, education, and scholarship. From the earliest days of P. T. Barnum and Cabinets of Curiosity, with their bearded ladies and Fiji mermaids grouped together with displays of artifacts from the past—a saltcellar holding the remains of Lot's wife and the ax that George Washington used to cut down the cherry tree[1]—the line between entertainment and education has remained blurry. Museums are driven by business imperatives that require robust visitation and financial security to justify their existence. Yet they are also seen by the public as inherently trustworthy and as guardians of a sacred trust—our concept of ourselves as a nation and as key transmitters of our civil society.[2]

Living history is a museum-based recreation of villages, cityscapes, or farms of the past populated by costumed staff members who portray characters from the time period represented. As will be seen, during its early days, living history was an extremely popular way to present history to the public in a uniquely contextual way. Initially, this formula was successful. Large East Coast examples of this type of museum, Colonial Williamsburg and Plimoth Plantation, experienced their zeniths during the 1970s. Their founders—often wealthy philanthropists who made their money in the industrial sector—typically set out to recapture a supposedly idyllic American past that reflected their values of thrift, hard work, and entrepreneurship. The villages, agricultural communities, and cities of the past were recreated as a paean to a past that only existed in their minds.[3] Despite this historical disconnect, most museum administrators truly did strive to present accurate depictions of the past. Studying these seeming contradictions and transformations through these institutional "histories of the presentation of history" is absolutely essential for museums today as they continue to try to carve out a place for themselves in the scarce leisure time of the American public.

Throughout the 1960s and 1970s, there was a burgeoning interest in public history from professional historians. Early academic writers on the topic emphasized the importance of providing context for visitors to museums so that the exhibits and reenactments were more accurate. In addition, museum theorists emphasized the importance of integrating best practices in research and historiography into the presentations to the public at museums.

Beginning in the mid-1980s, however, attendance at the leading living history museums like Colonial Williamsburg, Plimoth Plantation, Conner Prairie, and Greenfield Village at the Henry Ford Museum began to drop precipitously. Many solutions to this problem were tested by the leading museums, from devising new programs to streamlining operations, but no one solution staunched the flow of visitors away from living history museums.

Living history museums attempt to present honest portrayals of the past through accurate historical content. At the same time, these museums also need to entertain the public and be an attractive place for people to spend their leisure time. The tension and interplay between educational goals and entertainment is universal to all living history museums and will be explored here by examining both the history of public presentations at key examples of these museums and recent developments that continue to shape the landscape of museums in America. Public history can, at its best, inspire people to reflect on their own cultural situation and to learn more about the world around them. Learning theory has shown that this education is most effective when presented in an engaging, constructivist format.[4]

The huge upswing in interest around America's past in the mid-1970s is often viewed as the true beginning of living history in the United States. The fireworks of America's Bicentennial had barely cooled when program planners and historical interpreters (costumed staff portraying characters from the past) moved away from using the created past of living history as inspirational entertainment and focused instead on specific historically based content goals. By the late 1990s, this narrow focus estranged museums from their audience. More recently, the social milieu of the early 2000s, with personalized web-based interactions and increasing demographic fragmentation, caused museums to reexamine their tactics. Visitor evaluation and a data-based approach to understanding what visitors want from museums became a rallying cry for many of the change agent "magnetic" museums around the country.[5]

Museums today are listening to their visitors, actively engaging in co-creation, and working to become essential and trusted partners with communities. These trends are cast against the backdrop of the age-old push and pull of education and entertainment. It behooves us as museum professionals to take a closer look at where we came from in order to see where we might go.

History has already lost its relevance to much of the public. Roy Rosenzweig and David Thelen's *The Presence of the Past* (1998) showed that most Americans care deeply about their own personal connections with history—their genealogy and family stories—but that they are turned off by how museums and formal educators present history. These purveyors of the typically content-rich yet didactic and dull presentations of the past strip history of its vibrancy and relevance by deemphasizing relatable human stories and by using outmoded educational theories and techniques that may once have worked but are now as dead as the people that they try to teach about.

Museums must enter into the fray as equal players with the best experience providers out there. Borrowing good ideas from amusement parks, community groups, for-profit service providers, and the maker movement can only help as museums seek to prevent the leaky flow of visitors out of their doors. Amusing diversions are everywhere in our society, and museums must keep up. Museums are held in high respect by the public as trustworthy sources for information.[6] The most accurate research and authentic artifacts will be ignored if not shared in engaging and entertaining ways. We have the obligation not only to tell the right stories, but to also tell them so that people will listen.

NOTES

1. The ax handle has been replaced twice, and the ax head has been replaced once—but it's George Washington's original, the actual ax of George Washington!

2. "Public perceptions of—and attitudes to—the purposes of museums in society" (A report prepared by BritainThinks for Museums Association, March 2013), 3.

3. Jessica Swigger, "'History is Bunk': Historical Memories at Henry Ford's Greenfield Village" (Ph.D. diss., University of Texas at Austin, 2008), 94.

4. John H. Falk and Lynn D. Dierking, *Learning from Museums: Visitor Experiences and the Making of Meaning* (Walnut Creek, CA: AltaMira Press, 1996), 28.

5. Anne Bergeron and Beth Tuttle, *Magnetic: The Art and Science of Engagement* (Arlington, VA: American Alliance of Museums Press, 2013).

6. Roy Rosenzweig and David Thelen, *The Presence of the Past: Popular uses of History in American Life* (New York: Columbia University Press, 1998), 21.

2

PUTTING LIVING HISTORY IN CONTEXT

In this chapter, we will explore the history of living history museums. Throughout this section, we will contextualize why these museums became popular both in Europe and in North America and trace the various motivations for developing these museums. Let's start by traveling back to the 1880s to immerse ourselves in an example of living history in action.

STORY FROM THE FRONTLINES OF LIVING HISTORY

The homey-smelling kerosene lantern gave us light enough to locate the hook that latched the barn's main door. It had snowed heavily during the night, and a profound stillness pervaded the farmhouse and its outbuildings. I pushed aside enough snow to get to the cattle, who had gathered for warmth under the eaves. Using a wooden scoop, I filled a bucket with cracked corn, dust rising in puffs and filling the yellow lantern light with dancing motes.

Buttercup was hungry and ready to be milked. She rushed into the barn, mud swirling around her ankles, and immediately tucked into the corn in the trough. Attaching a lead to a metal ring on the side of the stall, I pulled a gleaming metal bucket between my feet and began to milk her. I set my brimmed leather hat on a peg after a few initial squirts and rested my head in the space between her belly and her hip. The warm, earthy smell of rich Jersey cow milk wafted through the milking parlor. The visitor who had paid $350 to stay for two nights at the farmhouse hadn't spoken. Neither had I. The spell of that peaceful morning was upon us.

I finally asked him if he wanted to give it a go, and I ceded the stool to him. We had given him and the rest of the participants a character biography and a brief description of the time period after we provided some basic orientation and safety tips (all in third-person, noncostumed attire). Now I was Fabius Schmidt, a farmhand who had recently gotten married and worked for the Zimmermans on their farm. In those moments, I had no trouble taking on a role. In some sort of strangely metaphysical way, I had transcended modern life and was fully in communion with the past.

We trudged back through the snow, the bucket sloshing milk and the sun just beginning to purple the sky. Pushing open the farmhouse door, the smell of freshly roasted coffee beans, frying bacon, and kerosene lent even more romance to the moment. But I was not in the late nineteenth century. I was only pretending. That morning was the closest I'd ever be to forgetting who I was. I knew that it wasn't sustainable in the long term. Ultimately, I was good at my job because I could navigate the modern mind and respond to visitor questions and needs using my historical knowledge and skills—not because I had somehow entered into the past and was living as if I actually was in that time period.

The example from Conner Prairie of these "Live In" programs brings to the fore the question of authenticity and artifice as methods of entertainment and education. The "Weekend on the Farm" (which was offered by Conner Prairie between 2004 and 2007) program attempted to immerse visitors in a time period (the 1880s in rural Indiana) and give them a role as a means to both providing an escape from the modern world and its hectic schedules and an experience that might lead to a deeper understanding of the past.[1] Woven through the entire experience was a storyline that gave the participants a chance to play a part in the past through relatable situations that mirrored contemporary problems. It was living history taken to its fullest immersive potential. But what were the antecedents of the "Weekend on the Farm" program that culminated in that milking parlor on a still winter morning in the mid-2000s?

THE ADVENT OF LIVING HISTORY

Living history museums are a relatively new phenomenon, but the desire to relive the "idyllic past" is a universal and age-old yearning. There is ample evidence, from Plato's Dialogues to escapist science fiction (which uses time machines as vehicles for social commentary about the depravity and inanity of modern society), that humans throughout history have desired to revisit the past "as it was." Additionally, people recreate history in ways that suit their own purposes.[2] A modern example of this is from Oliver Stone's 2004 film *Alexander*. Stone uses this film to try to persuade audiences that war is a great evil. History was merely a backdrop for his agenda. Recreated history often speaks more to the motivations of its creator than to the actual past. With these points in mind, it is not a far leap to understand the theoretical basis for living history museums. Creating fake towns, farms, and cityscapes is a way for people to understand themselves and the world around them as well as to experience a sense of nostalgia for a time that is perceived as more simple and pure.

One source that provides excellent insights into popular "constructions of the past" is historian David Lowenthal's *The Past Is a Foreign Country* (1985). Lowenthal emphasizes the importance of the past to humanity's present conception of itself. He argues that the desire to recapture an idyllic age inevitably leads to romanticization of the past. Lowenthal's thoughts in *The Past Is a Foreign Country* are further developed in an essay that he wrote that appeared in the book *History Museums in the United States: A Critical Assessment* (1990). In this chapter, he argues that pioneer museums are often considered to be the "least authentic" (authentic here seeming to refer to primarily "sticking to the facts") because they celebrate uniquely American myths.[3] In this same collection of essays, Michael Wallace contrasts "Disneyfied" history, where distortion of the past is acceptable as a means toward entertainment, with "real" history, which at its best seeks to propel people toward action as a way to learn from the past.[4] Wallace also argues that the past "is too important to be left to the private sector."[5] He continues to describe how corporations are beholden to profits and production and are not obligated to present aspects of history that might challenge their narratives of capitalism. As such, nonprofit museums are best positioned to affect change through stimulating action by providing more complete pictures of the past.[6] This supposition is tied together through his desire for a closer connection between scholarly and popular history in an effort to use public history to highlight the intersection between human agency and historical circumstances. He writes that "museums should consider it their fundamental mission to assist people to become historically-informed makers of history."[7]

Wallace's strong focus on museums' role in advocating for social and cultural change to bring about justice in society merits attention as it relates to living history. Living history museums in America, as conceived as purveyors of folklife and the stories of the "common man,"[8] have had a strong human agency core, where the pioneer spirit of people like William Conner to carve out a place for themselves in a difficult land was a key philosophical underpinning. Since the villages, homes, and farms were populated by interpreters dressed in historic clothing, the backstory and biography assigned to these characters made them fully formed human agents who did not follow a script to the letter and could share their dreams for the future with visitors. The historical circumstances that the interpreters found themselves in was then whatever time period given and the research into that time period that resulted in the material culture and setting of the site. In this context, a living history museum is perhaps the best example of good history. Living history museums, with their daily displays of the intersection of human agency and historical circumstances, provide a clear picture of a unique place and culture in a specific time.

EXAMPLES OF LIVING HISTORY IN THE UNITED STATES AND ABROAD

Roy Rosenzweig and David Thelen, in their 1998 work *The Presence of the Past*, demonstrate through extensive interviews with a wide cross-section of the country that many Americans are turned off by history as presented in the classroom setting and instead view museums and personal accounts from relatives or witnesses to historical events as being the most trustworthy source of information about the past.[9] They come to the conclusion that personal meaning making is the prime motivator for interest in history and that the national narratives that reigned in the historiography of the 1950s through the 1960s became less and less useful or relevant for most Americans as their sense of alienation with the government deepened during the 1960s and 1970s.[10] Rosenzweig and Thelen also posit that history museums are perhaps seen as so trustworthy because people often use museums as catalysts for developing identity and becoming more self-aware.

The didactic and expository educational theory in vogue at museums prior to the 1970s fed into their desire to showcase metanarratives. Places like Colonial Williamsburg and Plimoth Plantation, with their portrayal of critical nation-building moments, are excellent examples of this type of celebratory national history on display.[11] Experiential learning as a way to discover more about the past has been shown to be an important tool for museums as a way to promote self-awareness and reflection.[12] In addition, an understanding of the constructivist approach to learning, which acknowledges that people are not blank slates upon which information is written but are instead constantly combining new information with memories of prior experiences, impacted how museums presented the past to the public.[13] Museums such as Colonial Williamsburg and Plimoth Plantation that have an overtly national or political perspective may find it more difficult to pull away from their overarching narratives to break history into easily relatable, experiential nuggets that can spark visitors' curiosity.

Recent research into how children engage with the past has shown that imagination and creative play are key drivers for early entry into historical thinking and appreciation.[14] Learning theorists have rallied around experiential learning through engaging visitors' senses and immersing them in a time and place as the most effective ways to provide a gateway into the past to make history less abstract for young people.[15] The appeal of history museums to children is an important aspect of museums' continuing relevance in our society. The audience frequenting museums from the 1950s through the 1980s were primarily adult history enthusiasts who liked to travel to historical destinations out of a sense of civic and national pride or duty. As early as the mid-1990s, sociologists and commentators like Robert Putnam noted that civic and community organizations were slowly dying off as involvement in voluntary associations like the Lions Club dipped and the Greatest Generation (those who lived through World War II) was supplanted in numbers by Baby Boomers.[16] This newer audience had a variety of motivations for visiting museums, and a key driving force for many Baby Boomer parents (and now as grandpar-

Figure 2.1.   Reenactors converse in the pleasant surroundings of Colonial Williamsburg, circa 1980. Source: Photo by Carol M. Highsmith, courtesy of the Library of Congress.

ents) was (and is) to help provide experiences with the past for their children that are both fun and promote learning.[17]

An understanding of the importance of the social and interpersonal aspects of a museum visit is becoming more prevalent among public historians, with museums seen as being safe places for families to spend time with each other and build memories. History museums that have been able to change their audience focus to families with children have been better equipped to respond effectively to the downturn in museum visitation than those that continue to rely on civic-minded history enthusiasts as their core audience. As they widen their audience focus, living history museums have begun looking beyond the scope of what other history museums have done to provide experiences to guests and have started taking cues from children's museums, science centers, and even amusement parks as they seek to provide more varied and accessible experiences for family groups.

Interestingly, borrowing from amusement parks is a full-circle proposition for living history museums. Jessica Swigger, in her doctoral thesis about the development of the Henry Ford Museum and Greenfield Vil-

Figure 2.2.   A bold reenactor at Plimouth Plantation in Massachusetts surveys a historic building, circa 1980. Source: Photo by Carol M. Highsmith, courtesy of the Library of Congress.

lage outside of Detroit, explored at great length Walt Disney's visits to Greenfield Village in 1940 and 1948 that served as inspiration for Disneyland in southern California.[18] Disney was drawn to the nostalgia-laced and sanitized vision of America as presented at Greenfield Village and sought to reinvent amusement parks by creating one that provided the fun of fair rides, food, and a main street without the dirtiness and consumer excess that he saw at places like Coney Island. Both Disney and Henry Ford also sought to rid their respective utopias of the "troublesome" minorities, laborers, and liberated females that were becoming more prominent and vocal aspects of post-Depression society.[19] Ford's and Disney's recreations of idyllic pasts that were divorced from the reality of modern society spoke to their desire to enshrine and celebrate the traditional American ideals of democracy, frugality, patriotism, and white male domination. For those men, each of those ideals stood in opposition to the supposed threats of communist infiltration that dominated the popular and political zeitgeist of the 1950s.

Likewise, other historic sites like George Washington's birthplace became bastions of American ideals and values by riding the wave of the

Figure 2.3.   From left, Henry Ford, Thomas Edison, Warren Harding, and Harvey Firestone chat near a cabin that will eventually become part of the Firestone Farm at the Henry Ford Museum in 1921. Source: Photo by Harris and Ewing, courtesy of the Library of Congress.

virulent anticommunism of the Cold War. By presenting a supposedly truer picture of the past and the objects and inventors that made America what it was, historic sites could help to persuade the American public that democracy could be a bulwark against the anti-American forces of communism.

Other museums around the United States also became enamored of living history throughout the 1950s and 1960s; however, many of these were not labeled as such until the 1970s with the creation of the Association for Living History, Farm and Agricultural Museums (ALHFAM). With the new social history driving much of the focus on showcasing the history of regular people, even National Park Service sites began to catch on to living history during the 1970s. Seth Bruggeman, in his administrative history of the George Washington Birthplace National Monument, found that the development of living history at the site, while serving primarily to give visitors a glimpse into the everyday workings of an eighteenth-century plantation, was also a way for the museum to get maintenance work done by costumed interpreters using historic tools.[20]

Bruggeman also notes that 1970 was a pivotal year for interpretation at George Washington's birthplace, as the site sought to raise itself out of the controversial mire of two buildings with competing claims for authenticity as Washington's "true" birthplace.[21] The functionality of the landscape, manifested in living history displays of the historic agriculture, rare breeds, and trades of an eighteenth-century tidewater plantation, was given precedence over the memorializing house tours that typified pre-1970 interpretation at the site.[22]

The expanding number of living history museums throughout the 1960s and 1970s has also been viewed as a reaction to the decline of family farms during this time. Americans who held to the Jeffersonian ideal of small farms as the backbone of the country wanted to preserve the traditions of what they saw as a more pure and simple time. It is interesting to note that the 1950s saw both the largest single decade of exodus from rural areas to cities and a huge upswing in ardent anticommunism. In this sense, living history museums became part of the vanguard against the primarily city-centric countercultural movement.

LIVING HISTORY'S ORIGINS IN THE EUROPEAN
FOLKLIFE CENTERS

Similarly to America during the 1950s and 1960s, Scandinavia in the late 1890s was experiencing a time of questioning and of societal transition. Most early Scandinavian folklife recreations during the late 1800s set out to represent the past as it actually was and also to preserve the historical skills and trades of earlier times. In addition, these nascent museums often had political motivations. At the beginning of a 2005 interview with Conner Prairie Museum staff, Henry Glassie, professor of folklore at Indiana University, argued that Skansen, one of the most prominent living history museums in Sweden and the ancestor of folklife museums around the world, had an explicitly political frame of reference.[23] Glassie noted that Skansen's creator, Artur Hazelious, hoped that Skansen:

> [M]ight reverse time and might work against the homogeneousness of Sweden. [Hazelious] was thinking of not only displaying or preserving a few interesting Swedish things, [he] was interested in erecting a kind of bulwark against French culture that would allow . . . regular Swedish people to come and see it. [Hazelious] wanted the museum to become a part of an argument in the mind of the Swedish people about the Swedish destiny.[24]

Hazelious thus had an overtly political message in mind throughout the creation of Skansen. He was also transparent about the fact that he wove a political message through his historic site when he established it in the 1890s. Glassie was aware of the folklife model during the early conversations about the goals and ideas for Prairietown, the capstone living history site at Conner Prairie that opened to the public in the 1970s.

The founders and financiers of other living history museums, especially in the United States, also displayed political or cultural aims in their interpretations of history. Colonial Williamsburg in Virginia (which began significant restorations in 1928) and Greenfield Village in Dearborn, Michigan (begun in 1933), were both founded by wealthy men—John D. Rockefeller Jr. and Henry Ford, respectively—who wished to influence the public's perception of history. For Rockefeller, the industry and civic virtue of America's Founding Fathers merited a commemoration of their lives and times. Indeed, as Rockefeller wrote, Colonial Williamsburg would be a way for "the future to learn from the past."[25] For Ford, the preservation of the quickly decaying past was a way to educate the public about the importance of invention to the advance of industry and to train them to be patriotic citizens. [26] Both Colonial Williamsburg and Greenfield Village developed during the Great Depression and gained prominence through the Second World War. Rockefeller and Ford sought to idealize the past in order to boost Americans' view of themselves and to provide an escape from the harsh realities of the tough economic times and the engulfing struggles of the war. [27] Both Colonial Williamsburg and Greenfield Village were retreats from reality that claimed to be accurate and unfiltered depictions of the past.

Since any interpretation of the past is necessarily influenced by the biases of those doing the interpreting, any museum that claims that it presents the past "as it was" must be viewed warily. Hazelious, as a Swedish nationalist, used Skansen to argue that imported continental European culture should not be the highest ideal for the Swedish people. Skansen showed the traditional trades and lifestyles of the Swedish *volk* as worthy of remembrance and emulation in the present. [28] Rockefeller and Ford sought to deliver their message differently—both men enshrouded their political message in the rhetoric of authenticity. Visitors to these museums were supposed to think that they took a time machine into the past and could see an unbiased picture of what life was like in the time periods represented. Since the presentations at Colonial Williamsburg and Greenfield Village were sanitized and emphasized the stories of the wealthy, visitors must have left those museums with warped and decontextualized historical understanding.

Richard Handler and Eric Gable in *The New History in an Old Museum: Creating the Past at Colonial Williamsburg* explore how Rockefeller's "great man" approach to history had to go through a full makeover at Williamsburg after the social history of the 1970s transformed historiography. [29] Similarly, Henry Ford's approach of purchasing and then arranging historic homes and items from inventors from all over the country has been criticized by historians as creating a mishmash of decontextualized buildings at the Henry Ford Museum and Greenfield Village.

As social history emerged as a force among public historians, these museums became more willing to present history as encumbered with uncomfortable and challenging aspects of the past. In the case of Colonial Williamsburg and Greenfield Village, overcoming their challenging institutional history has been difficult, and both still struggle with their legacy of jingoist patriotism swaddled in supposedly neutral and authentic depictions of the past.

Philosophically, the planners of Conner Prairie fell somewhere between the tropes of authenticity pronounced by Ford and Rockefeller and Hazelious's explicit acknowledgment that history cannot be "objective." For Hazelious, history was a way for him to advance his political agenda. Eli Lilly was in part motivated in his initial decision to preserve the William Conner House by the desire to emphasize the enterprising spirit of early white settlers, whom he referred to as "pioneers," to Indiana.[30] Like Rockefeller and Ford, Lilly highlighted the importance of the prototypical American entrepreneur (typically seen as a white male pioneer who made a life for himself out of the "untamed wilderness") in shaping a quintessential American worldview. He also had similar goals of educating the public (with particular interest in character formation for youth) through explaining how people in the past were hard workers. Lilly used Conner's story because of his importance to the history of early central Indiana and because, out of sheer serendipity, he heard about the decaying "Conner House" from a friend.[31]

Evidence from correspondence between Lilly and various Conner Prairie stakeholders suggests that although Lilly began with this "great man" vision for his portrayal of Indiana's history, from a very early stage he hoped to portray the frontier experience of the common man.[32] Lilly's previous historical interests, as described in two books that he authored, one titled *The History of the Little Church on the Circle: Christ Church Parish Indianapolis 1837–1955* (published in 1957) and the other *Early Wawasee Days: Traditions, Tales, and Memories Concerning That Delectable Spot* (published in 1960), were focused on local, personal, and "regular" people, places, and events.[33] *Early Wawasee Days* "concentrated on the people—the Indians and first settlers and the fisherman, guides, hotelkeepers, sailors, and vacationing families;" in other words, the workaday people who formed the backbone of the Lake Wawasee region in northeastern Indiana.[34]

While this desire to showcase the regular people of history was clearly a part of Lilly's motivations for restoring buildings near Conner's home, Henry Glassie also postulated that Lilly was a "Hoosier Nationalist" who wanted "to celebrate what was true and native and fine about Indiana."[35] This perspective is corroborated by Lilly's charitable giving. Throughout his life he supported Indiana institutions that he felt represented the Hoosier spirit and ethos. Lilly's turn toward the common man approach could also boil down to the fact that since central Indiana did not have as many highly famous "great men," it was easier to place a stronger emphasis on more mundane history. Williamsburg in Virginia was a common haunt of Thomas Jefferson, and Ford was interested in bringing the homes of famous inventors like Thomas Edison and the Wright Brothers to his museum. Central Indiana was not able to showcase as many famous sons as Colonial Williamsburg and Greenfield Village.

Of course, all of these museums coupled their historical portrayals with a rich material culture. Eli Lilly did not furnish the buildings at Conner Prairie using evidence from the historical record.[36] Instead, to fill out the buildings, Lilly relied on his own personal taste and whatever he could find that looked like it could have fit the pioneer time period. Lilly was not unique in this mix-and-match approach to collecting and furnishing. During this time, many philanthropists, Ford and Rockefeller included, were hungry for nineteenth-century artifacts of all types, and feared that these items were rapidly being lost or ruined. They hoped to gather these items into collections before they were gone, and contextualization was not a high priority, to the detriment of the public.

The late 1960s and 1970s were times of profound disillusionment with government and the idea that America was essentially a righteous nation. Beginning in the late 1960s with racially driven urban riots, the dramatic expansion of the Vietnam War, and the general unrest of the country's youth, the change ushered in by these societal pressures affected all areas of American life.[37] The rise in the popularity of living history museums was one offshoot of these pressures.

Living history museums are reactionary to change and modernity. They ostensibly crystallize a moment in time for eternity. No matter what was going on in the world outside the walls (or split-rail fences) of the museum, at least the security of being able to step back into a time that was known and predictable remained. People could use living history museums to escape the change that they saw all around them. In the process, many walked away with the notion that life was simpler then and that they wished they could go back to that time permanently. Implicit in this type of mindset is the sentiment that the present has been corrupted by the forces of change.

As the bicentennial approached, many Americans had conflicting emotions about its meaning.[38] For some, it was merely a jingoistic celebration of the military prowess and superiority of the American people throughout history since its inception in 1776. For others, it signaled the decline of values over time. What had been a nation founded on principles of hard work and dedication to family and community had become so fragmented and dysfunctional by 1976 that for many, the bicentennial was a time for bittersweet and melancholic reminisce.

Living history museums wielded their greatest influence during the volatile crucible of the 1970s. Never again would living history museums have the type of robust attendance and respect of the public. The next chapter will explore how these carefully constructed "time machines" fell into decrepitude and disuse in the 1980s and 1990s.

NOTES

1. Do note that other museums implemented this type of in-depth immersion before Conner Prairie. The most notable are Norlands in Maine (a late nineteenth-century experience) and Pamplin Historical Park in Virginia, which immerses paying customers in Civil War soldier life.

2. David Lowenthal, *The Past Is a Foreign Country* (Cambridge: Cambridge University Press, 1985), 26.

3. David Lowenthal, "Pioneer Museums," in *History Museums in the United States: A Critical Assessment*, ed. Warren Leon and Roy Rosenzweig (Chicago: University of Chicago Press, 1990), 117.

4. Michael Wallace, "Mickey Mouse History: Portraying the Past at Disney World," in *History Museums in the United States: A Critical Assessment*, ed. Warren Leon and Roy Rosenzweig (Chicago: University of Chicago Press, 1990), 179. Wallace used the term "real" to describe history that was not beholden to corporate whims.

5. Ibid.

6. Michael Wallace, *Mickey Mouse History and Other Essays on American Memory* (Philadelphia: Temple University Press, 1996), 25.

7. Ibid.

8. The term "common man" here is one used primarily by social historians and the museum planners during the 1970s. Other terms that will be used interchangeably with "common man" are "ordinary people," "average man," and "regular people."

9. Roy Rosenzweig and David Thelen, *The Presence of the Past: Popular Uses of History in American Life* (New York: Columbia University Press, 1998), 21.

10. Ibid., 203.

11. Ibid., 127. Rosenzweig and Thelen make it clear that while white Americans had mostly positive associations with national metanarratives, African Americans and Native peoples were not as likely to have the same positive connotations.

12. George H. Hein and Mary Alexander, *Museums: Places of Learning* (Washington, DC: American Association of Museums Education Committee, 1998), 35.

13. John H. Falk and Lynn D. Dierking, *Learning from Museums: Visitor Experiences and the Making of Meaning* (Walnut Creek, CA: AltaMira Press, 1996), 28.

14. D. Lynn McRainey and John Russick, eds., *Connecting Kids to History with Museum Exhibitions* (Walnut Creek, CA: Left Coast Press, 2007), 119.

15. Ibid., 185.

16. Falk and Dierking, *Learning from Museums*, 211.

17. Robert D. Putnam, "Bowling Alone: America's Declining Social Capital," *Journal of Democracy* 6, no. 1 (January 1995): 65–79.

18. Jessica Swigger, "'History is Bunk': Historical Memories at Henry Ford's Greenfield Village" (Ph.D. diss., University of Texas at Austin, 2008), 94.

19. Ibid., 96.

20. Seth Bruggeman, "George Washington Birthplace National Monument: Administrative History, 1930–2000" (Williamsburg, VA: College of William and Mary, 2006), 176.

21. Seth Bruggeman, *Here George Washington Was Born: Memory, Material Culture, and the Public History of a National Monument* (Athens: University of Georgia Press, 2008), 171.

22. Ibid., 168.

23. Henry Glassie, interview by Timothy Crumrin, May 27, 2005, transcript, Conner Prairie Archive, 2.

24. Ibid.

25. Cary Carson, "Colonial Williamsburg and the Practice of Interpretive Planning in American History Museums," *Public Historian* 20, no. 3 (1998): 11–51.

26. Jay Anderson, *Time Machines: The World of Living History* (Nashville: AASLH Press, 1984), 28.

27. Sten Rentzhog, *Open Air Museums: The History and Future of a Visionary Idea* (Kristianstad, Sweden: Carlssons and Jamtli Press, 2007), 151.

28. Ibid., 122.

29. Richard Handler and Eric Gable, *The New History in an Old Museum: Creating the Past at Colonial Williamsburg* (Durham, NC: Duke University Press, 1997), 61.

30. Eli Lilly to Landrum Bolling, October 12, 1965, Conner Prairie Archive.

31. Ibid.

32. Henry Glassie, interview by Timothy Crumrin, May 27, 2005, transcript, Conner Prairie Archive, 15.

33. James H. Madison, *Eli Lilly: A Life, 1885–1977* (Indianapolis: Indiana Historical Society Press, 2006), 167.

34. Ibid., 168.

35. Henry Glassie, interview by Timothy Crumrin, May 27, 2005, transcript, Conner Prairie Archive, 16.

36. Madison, *Eli Lilly*, 175.

37. Bruce J. Schulman, *The Seventies: The Great Shift in American Culture, Society and Politics* (New York: The Free Press, 2001), 9.

38. By 1976, consensus historiography and a sense of the rightness of white national metanarratives had been obliterated by the Civil Rights movement and the growth of African American counternarratives. During the 1961–1965 Civil War Centennial, the national narrative was still entrenched with most historians and the majority of the white public. As Robert J. Cook points out in *Troubled Commemoration: The American Civil War Centennial, 1961–1965* (Baton Rouge: Louisiana State University Press, 2007), in 1960, the Civil War Centennial Commission set out to convey to the public that the Civil War "had been a collective, national experience" and that the centennial was a time to celebrate the unity between the North and the South that arose in the aftermath of the war (41). Cook argues that as the Civil Rights movement challenged this white-centric understanding of the Civil War and its aftermath with regard to the African American experience, the public's perception on the meaning of the war changed as well (273).

3

MAKING MEANING AND CREATING AUTHENTICITY AT MUSEUMS

Authors with intimate knowledge of their subject have both an advantage and a challenge. Their familiarity can swing toward celebratory hagiography that ends up sounding false and aggrandizing or it can reveal layers of meaning that show the subject in new, surprising ways. My hope is that this section ends up avoiding the potential pitfalls and becomes an illuminating glimpse at a highly unique and innovative time at Conner Prairie Interactive History Park.

STORY FROM THE FRONTLINES OF LIVING HISTORY

Limping out of a year in the classroom as a history and government teacher, I applied to work at Conner Prairie as a part-time interpreter—a gig, I thought, that would keep the money coming in over the summer as I looked for another job in teaching. Unlike many museum professionals, I had never really had a "conversion experience" when I knew that all I wanted to do was work in museums. Instead, I stumbled into museum work as an accident. My ignorance of the daily lifeways of the past that are so valued at living history museums was deep. On my first day I blurted out something like, "Should I start growing a beard or what?" Foolish me. The 1830s (the time period for the Prairietown village) were a clean-shaven time. Beards were viewed as uncouth and profane, and hirsute gentlemen were often castigated as wannabe hermits or slovenly rascals. The trainer (an expert in nineteenth-century fashion and clothing) kindly corrected my misperception as I came to the growing realization that this living history thing was going to be a much different beast than the "book learnin'" that I was used to.

Conner Prairie in 2002 was in a growth phase. With a director[1] focused on shaking the museum out of a decade-long period of stasis, a new professional corps of managers and coordinators had been hired to push Conner Prairie in a different direction. Many of these new hires were midcareer graduates of museum studies programs who had been at other living history museums prior to being hired at Conner Prairie.

My training class was the typical mixture of college kids, recent graduates, and retirees. Training lasted five days and was mostly held in classrooms inside the museum, with only occasional forays to the historic grounds and public areas. Much of the content focused on discrete nuggets of history from the time periods portrayed at the museum: 1830s foodways, 1830s politics, 1830s agriculture, 1830s cultural norms—you get the idea. Sprinkled in were a few opportunities to practice communication skills and to get to know the audience coming to the museum. My most salient memory, however, is getting a lesson in wood splitting and then getting to try it out.

After this "Basic Training" (that was its actual name), we were placed in our first areas. I ended up in Pastport, a Prairietown-lite with a candle-dipping station, a Breeds and Seeds area with a sheep or a horse grazing and lazing nearby, Tools of the Trade with a froe and a mallet and a draw knife and shave horse (and, of course, innumerable scrap pieces of wood), and Hearth and Home with a cabin with "the only bed at Conner Prairie that you can actually sit on" and a loom. This area was interpreted in third person, with a focus on narrowly defined hands-on activities.

In my early days at Conner Prairie, I scrapped for all the hours that I could and constantly volunteered to be trained in new areas or to work the least desirable shifts—the watermelon seed spitting station on July 4 ranks up there on the nastiness meter. Throughout this time, I kept my eyes on the interpretive prize and the highest aspiration for most part-time staff—working in Prairietown as a first-person interpreter. Seen as the most challenging job at the museum, I knew that I would be able to learn the most and would have more chances to show my mettle and possibly get a full-time job if I could get into Prairietown. I'd also be able to wear some natty 1830s clothes.

The day arrived in mid-July. I rummaged through the historic clothing room and located a pair of tight gray trousers, a green flower-print waistcoat, a blindingly white linen shirt, and a red-checked neckerchief. I topped all this with a floppy-brimmed black felt hat. After morning briefing, I hitched myself to the most senior and content-knowledgeable interpreter whom I'd already shadowed for two days wearing "plainclothes." This was my third day of training and I was Peter Dale, Doctor Campbell's apprentice.

The air was already hot and moist as I turned the corner and headed toward the yellow house at the heart of the village. Verdant green trees and tangles of underbrush pulsed at the edges of the wide dirt road. Two hefty slate gray oxen lowed with a crackling intensity from behind a split rail fence as we passed. I could feel the transforming sense of stepping into another time taking over. Then a golf cart came ripping by, piloted by a Carhart-clad guy who tossed a few flakes of hay from the back of the cart to the livestock and then peeled out and away. It didn't take long to break the spell.

The Campbell house was large enough to warrant posting three or four staff in different areas of the house—typically Doctor Campbell's acerbic aunt, who was visiting the backwater of Prairietown from the far more cosmopolitan Lexington, Kentucky, or Mrs. Campbell positioned in the parlor. Then the Campbell's cook in the kitchen (naturally) and Doctor Campbell or his apprentice Peter Dale set up in the office. Upon arriving "on post," we met as a team to devise the plan for the day—when we would take our lunches and breaks, what the person in the kitchen planned on cooking, and a brief snippet from the news for that particular day in 1836 (the "massacre" at the Alamo down in Texas was a germane topic that year).

It wasn't long before the first visitors of the day arrived. During Basic Training, a few senior staff intimated that visitation during the summer was generally more low-key than the spring and fall, which featured scads of fourth graders[2] and all the busyness that school groups bring. I felt more than ready to interpret the past on my first day on the historic grounds. I hadn't had to learn a trade like carpentry or blacksmithing, and I would be evaluated on my ability to convey a list of "post goals" that lined up with specific historic content to visitors. For Peter Dale, that meant talking about medicine in the 1830s—house calls versus visiting a doctor's office, for example—and the economy of small towns during that era.

I had a few items at my disposal to help bring these content goals to life. Doctors during the pioneer era often served as de facto dentists, so the office had a tooth key to show how extraction worked. The tooth key was a small wooden-handled device with a hinged arm that could be wedged around a tooth and then, with a simple (and excruciatingly painful) twist and pull, the tooth would pop out. I also had some cloth bandages that I could let kids roll and a surgery kit complete with a bone saw and some wicked-looking rusty knives. Arrayed on the shelves behind me were glass bottles and vials with labels—"quinine" (malaria medicine) and "leeches" (for removing the bad humors) were the most intriguing.

Every character in Prairietown had an extensive backstory. Some of these could go on for dozens of pages and were filled with details about where the character came from, how they got to Prairietown, what their hopes for the future were, and why their relationships with other people in the village were so cantankerous or so congenial. Peter Dale was trying to earn money to attend a college to learn more about medicine. He also slept on the floor of the doctor's office on a straw tick. As most interpreters do, I embellished the backstory to try to make the character more relatable. The real advantage of human-to-human interaction at museums lies in the ability to make meaningful connections with visitors and build a rapport that will open the door to curiosity in a rich way. My favorite moments as Peter Dale were always ones where, for at least a few moments, I was able to elicit some measure of empathy or compassion.

Stories are the fuel for the flame of human empathy and understanding. Our lives adhere to a narrative arc (we are born, we live in a place and time, we die) and narratives have the power to sculpt our perception of ourselves and others in profound ways. The best types of history interpretation tell good stories. In museums, as far back as Freeman Tilden in *Interpreting our Heritage* (1957), compelling stories compellingly told have been the benchmark for successful experiences at museums. From a foundation of interesting human stories, museums can create relatable narratives that build toward deeper understanding and empathy toward those who lived in the past and, hopefully, create pathways toward solutions to current societal challenges. But how did Conner Prairie strike on this approach to interpreting the past as the more efficacious way to communicate history?

CONNER PRAIRIE BEFORE 2002

During the height of the Depression, Eli Lilly, Indianapolis's pharmaceutical leader and philanthropist, employed Tillman Bubenzer, a down-on-his-luck German immigrant, to run an experimental farm. It lay across the White River from a newly restored brick house of minimal historic import.[3] At that time, Lilly hoped that new and improved breeds of hogs and cattle would advance Indiana's stature as a leading hub of agricultural innovation. In the following years, Lilly's venture failed to recognize profits and, by 1967, it was losing money. His small brick house of minimal historic import, however, was quietly drawing visitors from around the state. They walked through its pioneer-themed rooms (the house was built in 1823) and looked out from its windows over the same floodplain that settler William Conner once looked across.[4] Lilly and the administrators of the recently christened "Conner Prairie" saw that the almost 1,500-acre money-losing expanse of land could become something more than a small historic house museum surrounded by fancy hogs and barren silos.

James Madison, in his biography of Eli Lilly, describes Lilly's disdain for the rising materialism and self-centeredness in the America of the 1940s and 1950s; this concern also helps to explain Lilly's investment in Conner Prairie. Concurrent to his burgeoning interest in historic preservation, Lilly became enamored with the writings of two sociologists. One of these, a nebbish Russian-born sociologist named Pitirim Sorokin, warned that America was in crisis and that the only remedy for the materialism of the age was a return to the values embodied in Christ's Sermon on the Mount.[5] The other, Ernest M. Ligon, also focused his writings on the Sermon on the Mount, but with a special emphasis on its power to transform the character of children from their earliest years. Lilly invested substantially (both financially and with his time) in Sorokin's and Ligon's projects and initiatives throughout the 1950s and 1960s. Despite these investments and his initial enthusiasm for their work, Lilly eventually became disillusioned with a lack of tangible results. Examining Lilly's correspondence with Landrum Bolling, a close friend and the president of Earlham College (located in Richmond, Indiana) during this time, makes clear that by the early 1970s, Lilly began to shift his focus away from the sociologists' initiatives and toward Conner Prairie's potential to

Figure 3.1.   This image shows a diagram of the Conner Farm from 1933 from the Historic American Buildings Survey. The contemporaneous text accompanying this image says, "Significance: An interesting group of restored buildings on an early Indiana farm, including the first brick house in the 'New Purchase' of Indiana, which comprised roughly the central third of Indiana." Note that the numeral one in this diagram is the William Conner House and the farm structures are located to the rear and north of the historic house. What is now Prairietown at Conner Prairie Interactive History Park is located to the south (out of frame) of numerals two and three. Source: Diagram by Historic American Buildings Survey, courtesy of the Library of Congress.

help a wider audience understand the importance of returning to the morals of scripture, upon which he believed our country was founded.

Although Lilly never expressed this view explicitly, it seems clear from his interest in character development that he viewed the recreations of the past at Conner Prairie as a way to share the values of a more frugal, honest, and biblically rooted time. When, in 1969, Lilly gave Earlham College forty thousand shares of stock in his company, he specified that the gift was to be used "to operate the Conner Prairie Farm Museum complex . . . on a basis which will effectively and appropriately communicate to young people and to the general public the record of Indiana's early history."[6] The important phrase here that connects his interest in Sorokin's and Ligon's work with what he hoped Conner Prairie would accomplish is "young people." By specifically calling attention to this demographic group, Lilly emphasized the importance that he placed on character development for youth.

As Prairietown took shape in the 1970s, Lilly made frequent visits to the museum to check on the progress of construction or to take in a lesson at the "country schoolhouse."[7] His satisfaction with the direction of the museum during its formative period, as evidenced by increased financial support, shows that Conner Prairie was using the recreation of the past to contrast modern values with the idyllic character of Indiana's pioneers. Harold Cope, Earlham's business manager in 1970, said as much in a revealing statement to a joint meeting of the Conner Prairie Advisory Council and the Earlham Board of Trustees. It is worth quoting in full:

> With increased leisure time and growing population many opportunities present themselves in the field of education outside the areas of formal instruction. Our young people, above all other things, are searching for an identity and a purpose. Whether they know it or not, they hunger for situations where they can step outside their normal life and seek for a different perspective. Many of them have never seen the process of making an article from raw material. Many have never seen or experienced the dignity of work or the pleasure of a simple, slower-paced way of life. Here is what Conner Prairie can contribute. We can transport the individual back in time, and at a slower pace, demonstrate the virtues and strengths upon which our present society has been constructed . . . to understand that his fore-fathers had a hard, but not unsatisfactory life, and one which does not always conform to our present day ideals and aspirations.[8]

A key insight here from Cope is his statement that young people are "searching for an identity and purpose." Against the backdrop of change that characterized America in the late 1960s, Cope set Conner Prairie as a remedy for young people's perceived aimlessness and ennui. Middle-class young people of the 1960s had an unprecedented amount of disposable income and free time and were choosing to express themselves through consumption and conspicuous materialism.[9]

Spiro Agnew, the blustery vice president of the United States under Richard Nixon between 1969 and 1973, said in a speech in 1969 that "the young . . . at the zenith of physical power and sensitivity, overwhelm themselves with drugs and artificial stimulants. Subtlety is lost, and fine distinctions based on acute reasoning are carelessly ignored in a headlong jump to a predetermined conclusion."[10] He continued, "The lessons of the past are ignored and obliterated in a contemporary antagonism known as the generation gap. A spirit of masochism prevails, encouraged by an effete corps of impudent snobs who characterize themselves as intellectuals."[11]

Rhetoric of this sort about countercultural youth was a hallmark of the establishment representatives of the "Greatest Generation," which so rued many of the rapid changes taking place in America.

Cope echoes Agnew as he sets the 1960s in context even more stridently in a later part of the same statement quoted above: "Old patterns of living and values are being challenged. . . . The ideals, mores and religions of our Society are being questioned, investigated, and discussed. No aspect of our lives is considered sacred, or above scrutiny by our younger generation."[12] The antidote to the questioning and searching for purpose, from Cope's perspective, was that if countercultural youth could see the "dignity of work" and the "slower pace" of life in the past, they would be more likely to strive to be productive members of society. By extension, they would also be more willing to conform to the pioneer values if they could experience them in an informal setting that *showed* them how average people lived instead of merely *describing* how they lived.

The history experience at living history museums is formed in the interaction between the museum's interpreters and the public, sharing stories as I did as Peter Dale in Prairietown. The importance of that information as constructed rather than received points to a critical aspect of how interpretation works at museums. We need to look at how the public experiences their visits and not at simply the message promoted by museum professionals. In doing so, we can determine to what extent historical education can be gained there.

CREATING MEANING AT MUSEUMS

David Glassberg in *Sense of History* writes that "every person is his or her own historian, creating idiosyncratic versions of the past that make sense based on personal situation and experience."[13] Visitors to museums, then, are not just passive recipients of the information presented, but are rather continually constructing their own meanings into what they are seeing. Clearly, however, the way that museums present the history and the prejudices and biases they bring to the design process will affect the meaning that individuals construct for themselves. Glassberg's analysis supports this idea. He continues, "But our individual memories are not solely the product of idiosyncratic recollection; they are also established and confirmed through dialogue with others."[14]

One assumption that professionals bring to their push to contextualize history and show how visitors construct meaning is an understanding that all presentations of the past necessarily involve some aspect of "invention." Because museums can never exactly replicate a place in time "as it was," approximations of the past that educate the public through entertaining, invented vignettes and stories are the most stimulating way to present history.

Examinations of how visitors constructed meaning at living history museums were rife during the mid-1980s. The "golden age" of living history museums (the time right around the Bicentennial) was beginning to wane, but historians were still grappling with how public history could help visitors get a better grasp on historical concepts. Social historians who advocated for using objects to tell the stories of specific cultural groups and communities began to advocate for using museums to explore multiple perspectives as a way to understand societal pressures and debates. Colonial Williamsburg (and other living history museums of its ilk) felt that their emphasis on authenticity and showing history in its social totality "as it actually was" gave them a moral high ground in this debate.

The cover of a glossy mid-1980s coffee table book of photos taken at Colonial Williamsburg has a telling statement that provides a glimpse at this perspective in action: "Today Colonial Williamsburg remains a pioneer in its field, continuing . . . to present an ever more faithful portrait of life in our ancestor's time."[15] By the 1990s, the "faithful portrait" of the past included what Handler and Gable described as "authenticity [as] Colonial Williamsburg's mission" that sought to portray "the history of previously excluded people such as African American slaves, and the social history of consumerism, of the material culture of everyday life."[16] The gritty authenticity that living history museums tried to achieve in theory often hit a tense reality when one-on-one interactions between interpreters and visitors take place. The controversial and painful aspects of the past (domestic violence, racism, slavery, sexism, child labor, and unsanitary conditions) are often neglected or scarcely mentioned at living history museums because they tend to make visitors feel uncomfortable when they are trying to enjoy leisure time.

The tension between discomfort and entertainment are vividly on display in an interview with an interpreter at Colonial Williamsburg who said, "In academia you can ask probing questions that will make people uncomfortable. You do not have that sanction in a museum that is . . . here to entertain people and help people feel good."[17] This supposed tension is based on a faulty assumption. It actually is possible to present history that challenges the public without making them feel unduly uncomfortable. We will explore how guests can both enjoy an intellectually and physically comfortable experience at the museum and how simultaneously their preconceptions can be challenged by delving into the concept of authenticity in the next section.

AUTHENTICITY IN LIVING HISTORY MUSEUMS

Perhaps the commonality between amusement parks like Disney World and history museums lies in the telling of good human stories. Disney (the corporation), as a purveyor of comfortable and fun experiences, tells good stories. So can historians. It just so happens that the stories told by historians are based on documentary evidence. Disney romanticizes the past in order to give people what they think they want and expect. History museums tend to try to recreate the past more honestly and full of the warts and difficulties that make the past so messy and, ultimately, so fascinating.

The struggle between presenting accurate and inclusive history and entertaining presentations to the public has been a constant theme for living history museums. The medium is so unique and fraught with pitfalls that the most common explanations to justify its paradoxes are arguments that try to describe what living history museums are not. Museum professionals have been known to visibly shudder at the word "Disney." Any comparisons to or potential lessons from the theme park industry are typically met with derision and revulsion. But, as Tity DeVries writes in her case study about Alaska's Pioneer Park titled "Ambiguity in an Alaskan Theme Park: Presenting 'History as Commodity' and 'History as Heritage,'" the park's "location is not historically authentic and most of its buildings and attractions were relocated from elsewhere . . . making money from the park was considered more important than preserving Fairbanks' heritage."[18] Similarly, the motivations for creating Conner Prairie also included a desire to, if not actually make money, at least break even. Conner Prairie management during its formative years as a living history museum recognized the balance that both breaking even and keeping true to the historical record would entail: "while we definitely do not want a tourist trap, people are looking for interesting things to do."[19]

When interested tourists come to experience the past at living history museums, they do so in a specific spot of land. This land has been populated with a network of meanings and perspectives meant for public consumption. Some historians have attempted to synthesize public history with landscape and environmental history. Elizabeth Kryder-Reid examined how the designs of Catholic missions in California serve very specific interests. She argues that though these missions are portrayed for tourists as beautiful expressions of Catholicism, they were historically oppressive vehicles of colonization.[20]

As seen in the example of California missions, those in power greatly influence how the public perceives the meaning of a physical space— even if the meaning of the space is contested. Patricia West in *Domesticating History: The Political Origins of America's House Museums* (1999) also explores this phenomenon by showing how the interpretation at Colonial Williamsburg and Greenfield Village reflected middle-class male-centric values when philanthropists and male architects took over the governance of those sites from women's associations in the early twentieth century.[21] Conner Prairie's origins are slightly different, in that when Eli Lilly purchased the property it had never been administered as a historical monument. However, Lilly did align himself with Rockefeller's and Ford's approach through his hope that "the buildings and artifacts of frontier America would build character in modern Americans who saw them."[22]

Parsing out the various motivations for recreating a specific time and place (whether to enforce a specific political or societal agenda, to make money, or to challenge previously held visitor assumptions about the past) highlights a critical juxtaposition for museums and historic sites. On one hand, museums have an obligation (as purveyors of history and the "power wielders" who portray the past to a trusting public) to be as accurate as possible in their interpretations of the past, even to the extent of presenting uncomfortable historical situations.[23] On the other, museums must continue to pay the bills and draw enough visitors to stay solvent and maintain their endowment. Historians such as Michael Wallace have often presented these two as inherently at odds with each other

in the museum world.[24] But an analysis of recent trends in living history
and first-person interpretation complicates this understanding and allows
us to see that tension as not inevitable. The next section will explore the
many ways that museums have found unique methods to present the often
uncomfortable past to the public using both entertaining and educational
techniques.

LIVING HISTORY IN ACTION

Like a good superhero yarn, origin stories for museums often involve a
transformation and a galvanizing trial that spurs the museum toward new
heights. For Conner Prairie, this involved the experimental farm that
continued to lose money year after year. Eli Lilly would write a check at
the end of the fiscal year to cover the amount that Tillman Bubenzer, his
farm manager, had lost during the year.[25] Lilly had given Earlham College in Richmond, Indiana, a substantial endowment to provide for the
Conner House's continued maintenance "in perpetuity."[26]

Over the course of the first few years after the initial transfer of the
property to Earlham, nothing much changed physically at Conner Prairie.
Earlham sought guidance from consultants and advisory committees
while Bubenzer and his wife continued to give tours to interested individuals and school groups at the Conner House. During this time, administrators decided to separate Lilly's farm operation from the museum operation. Stemming from discussions with these various advisory boards,
Earlham's president, Landrum Bolling, proposed that there were three
courses of action that the college could take concerning the gift from
Lilly. Two of the options involved doing little more than maintaining the
property and continuing with limited hours of operation for the public.
The third option, however, had "a goal of making it [Conner Prairie] the
type of educationally attractive historical center that would be both educational and entertaining, and would hopefully produce income sufficient
to cover all expenses and possibly show a profit."[27]

With the goal of creating an educational and entertaining historical
center that would transform Conner Prairie into a more broad-based am-
bitious museum, the Earlham board hired a full-time museum director
(Richard A. Sampson) and set him loose. Upon hiring him, they encouraged him to take into account the landscape of the site, the potential for

visitorship from the surrounding areas, and the existing resources and expertise of administrators and staff at Earlham.[28]

Sampson's initial plan to bring in buildings to the site to recreate Indianapolis circa 1825 was scuttled. Objections to this plan included the prickly fact that recreating a city that actually existed forty miles south of the site would most likely be confusing to the public.[29] Some board members felt that the rural landscape of the area was worth preserving. They argued that using the museum to interpret rural and "small town" history was a more efficacious approach.

Eventually the board decided to hire an outside firm to conduct a feasibility study for the site.[30] By 1970, the consulting firm, James and Berger Associates, Henry Glassie (the avuncular folklore and vernacular architecture theorist from Indiana University), and Conner Prairie staff began to ready the stage for the performance. The land that became the living history village of Prairietown had been bucolic farmland for many years. In 1970, Tillman and Louisa Bubenzer lived in a farmhouse on a bluff overlooking the White River's floodplain to the south of the Conner House. Before the Bubenzer's and Lilly arrived, William Conner's descendants and a string of absentee landlords had farmed fields of corn and created paddocks for livestock on that land. Before Conner chose that spot of land to build his house, the floodplain was farmed by Native Americans, who chose that location because they could farm the land without having to clear any trees and there was plentiful water from the river nearby.[31] In 1970, for the first time in the history of that particular place, people decided to self-consciously create a village that had never existed there. The land was no longer used for practical purposes. Food production and habitation became vignettes within the play of living history. The land was estranged from the visceral reality of survival that agricultural and shelter represent.

Environmentalists have long argued that golf courses and cemeteries are two of the biggest wastes of land and water resources in the United States. Museums and historic sites have traditionally fought back against the claim that inefficient old buildings waste resources, arguing that by continuing to use and occupy these spaces, they are in fact the "ultimate recycling" due to the energy that has already been invested throughout their long existence.[32] Conner Prairie, in this case, aligned itself with the idea that recycling old buildings was actually the best path toward helping the public better understand historical and environmental causations.

An interesting anecdote that connects Bubenzer's work on Lilly's Conner Prairie Farm to the living history museum that took its place comes from an article about Bubenzer's management in a winter 1956 issue of *The Farm*, an agricultural trade magazine. In this fascinating piece, which was published in the midst of a surprisingly profitable two years at the experimental farm, the writer describes Bubenzer thusly:

> Having been born in Imperial Germany and worked under conditions of rigid class distinction, it is not surprising to find Bubenzer intensely interested in preserving democracy here. The importance of individual liberty and the economy which makes this possible is a theme he manages to get into almost every discussion. When he talks of this new breeding boar project he says, in an accent that seems more French than German, "We feel that the farmer-owned farm which is so important to our way of life is being threatened because the livestock are inefficient converters of feed into meat. We feel challenged to produce an efficient, meat-type hog that will help the farmer increase the number of pigs he markets and reduce the feed it takes to bring them to market weight."[33]

Efficient swine serving as agents of democracy sounds dubious on the surface, but Bubenzer's desire to create the best hog, regardless of pedigree, is certainly echoed by Lilly's desire to portray the "pioneer spirit" of the early settlers to Indiana, who came from humble origins, yet worked together to create the best situation for themselves in the hardscrabble wilderness.

1956, the year that this article was written, saw two of the more "hot" events of the Cold War burst into the public consciousness—the Suez Canal crisis and the Hungarian uprising. Both of these events laid bare the tensions between the democratic United States and the communist USSR. Perhaps *The Farm*'s emphasis on advancing democracy through agriculture is reflective of the heightened fear of communism during this time. Additionally, the post–World War II flight from farms and small towns to cities was a daily pressure on traditional values of the sort that Lilly and Bubenzer would have supported.

PRAIRIETOWN'S PHILOSOPHICAL FOUNDATION

Myron Vourax, Conner Prairie's director during the mid-1970s, wanted to build Prairietown to drive attendance.[34] He realized that visitors wanted to see people dressed in costumes and "living" in 1836. Vourax perceived the success of the museum as being tied to its ability to draw the public to the site through presenting an entertaining product.

In 1975, Vourax presented a paper entitled "The Conner Prairie Concept" to the Association for Living History, Farm and Agricultural Museums' annual meeting. In it, he described Conner Prairie's core mission:

> For "education" of people to succeed   for their minds to be changed by the Conner Prairie experience—they must be in part entertained on the tour. People can't be told the tour is going to be "educational"—because few come to a restoration to be educated. People want to be entertained. Education through entertainment is the key to a successful tour experience at Conner Prairie Pioneer Settlement.[35]

Elsewhere in this document, Vourax emphasized the importance of being able to fictionalize the past to educate. He compared the Conner Prairie approach to a work of art: "The purpose of . . . art work is to get the viewer's attention in order to convey a message, a vision, a point of view. We select facts which convey a powerful impression of the reality of past living."[36] The goal was not to strictly recreate what life was like in 1836, but rather to give a flavor of the time period through representative buildings, artifacts, storylines, and environments. An important point here is that the facts selected make all the difference in what the "reality of past living" ends up looking like. To return to Kryder-Reid's argument, those in power determine the stories that are told and the facts that are used. As will be shown, in some cases stories that could have been explored were neglected in creating Prairietown.

Vourax and Eli Lilly had a shared understanding of what authenticity meant in a living history setting. When Prairietown was dedicated on March 31, 1974, some of those theories were described to an audience comprising numerous dignitaries, including then mayor of Indianapolis, Richard Lugar, and the lieutenant governor of Indiana, Robert Orr. On that chilly but bright spring day, the program for the ceremonies began by restating Conner Prairie's "commitment to portray the realities of early Indiana."[37] After affirming that William Conner's life was still an essential part of the stories that the museum told, it continued: "As we expand the number of buildings and the scope of the interpretation, one thing will remain constant with us—our determination that every architectural detail, each craft product, every explanation by a guide is completely true to the past."[38] Authenticity, then, was defined as being "true to the past" in everything that the public encountered in Priarietown. From the buildings themselves to those who "lived" in the buildings and talked to visitors, the entirety of the experience should have given this sense of truthfulness to the historical record. Since truthfulness was the goal, it is helpful to examine what living history does best to show where it succeeds and where it often fails in being truthful to the historical record.

Living history interpretation lends itself much more naturally to object- and environment-focused presentations—the "architectural details" and "craft products" described in the dedication program. More abstract processes like government, religious beliefs, and race relations are much tougher to portray through the "explanations by guides." The uses of guides (who are variously called interpreters, first-person characters, actors, and enactors) in living history museums represents a shift away from a strictly artifact- and exhibit-driven approach to interpretation at museums.

The people portraying the composite characters meant to embody people who would have actually lived in the 1830s are fully of their own (subsequent) time period. As such, they have all of the thought patterns and cultural baggage of the modern era along with the comfort of knowing that they can get in their car and go home to air conditioning when their shift is over. No matter how hard interpreters try to inhabit the nineteenth-century mindset, they cannot escape the modern reality in which they actually exist. The story from the Weekend on the Farm experience at the beginning of chapter 2 is a prime example of how even when the environment and situation were fully in place to immerse me into a time and place, I never truly forgot that I was a Generation X museum worker.

This juxtaposition showed itself in some of the early attempts at first-person interaction at Conner Prairie. This character-driven dialogue approach as a way to communicate history ended up often being a scatter-shot affair, with different techniques frequently applied. John Schippers, one of the first craftsmen hired to help build Prairietown, wrote, "We, in the beginning, did try a lot of experimenting with our new first person interpretation and we did make a lot of mistakes."[39]

The origins of the widespread use of first-person interpretation at museums are rather murky, although many museums, from Colonial Williamsburg to National Parks Service sites, did experiment with it in some form as early as the 1960s.[40] By 1977, however, only Plimoth Plantation, under the guidance of James Deetz, had explored installing systematic first-person characterizations as the primary mode of communication to visitors at a museum.[41]

Sometimes the more illuminative way to shine a light on how living history's past might inform its present is to hear firsthand from current practitioners and champions of it. The next chapter will explore some case studies from museums that challenge and engage visitors, while at the same time being fully embraced as comfortable, familiar places.

NOTES

1. John Herbst, Conner Prairie Director from 1999 to 2004.

2. All public school fourth graders study Indiana history, so history museums like Conner Prairie typically see lots of school groups as a result.

3. William Conner, who built the house, was one of the first white men to settle in Hamilton County, Indiana. He was an Ohio-born merchant who made his living from trade with the local Native American peoples (in particular the Lenape, also known as the Delaware) who had settled along the White River. Conner served several nonconsecutive and undistinguished terms as a state legislator. He later took up residence in Noblesville, Indiana, Hamilton County's seat. Conner certainly had an interesting life and was an important figure in the development of Hamilton County and central Indiana, but his broader significance to the rest of the state and to the nation was minimal at best. The early interpretations of the Conner story are an interesting story in their own right, but will not be discussed here. See chapter 3 of David B. Allison's "Entertaining the Public to Educate the Public at Conner Prairie: Prairietown 1975 to 2006," (IUPUI MA diss., 2010). It has more information about these early depictions of William Conner.

4. Landrum Bolling to Eli Lilly, July 15, 1967, Conner Prairie Archive, Fishers, IN. (Hereafter "Conner Prairie Archive" will be referred to as CP Archive.)

5. James H. Madison, *Eli Lilly: A Life, 1885–1977* (Indianapolis: Indiana Historical Society Press, 2006), 193.

6. "Deed of Gift by Eli Lilly to Earlham College," January 24, 1969, CP Archive.

7. Madison, *Eli Lilly*, 267.

8. "Director's Statement to Joint Meeting of the Conner Prairie Advisory Council and the Earlham Board of Trustees," April 18, 1970, Earlham College Archive, Richmond, IN.

9. Christopher Lasch, *The Culture of Narcissism: American Life in an Age of Diminishing Expectations* (New York: W. W. Norton and Company, Inc., 1978), 71.

10. Spiro Agnew, Speech on October 1969, from *In Our Own Words: Extraordinary Speeches of the American Century*, ed. Senator Robert Torricelli and Andrew Carroll (New York: Washington Square Press, 1999), 286.

11. Ibid.

12. "Director's Statement to Joint Meeting of the Conner Prairie Advisory Council and the Earlham Board of Trustees," April 18, 1970, Earlham College Archive, Richmond, IN.

13. David Glassberg, *Sense of History: The Place of the Past in American Life* (Amherst: University of Massachusetts Press, 2001), 9.

14. Ibid., 10.

15. Phillip Kopper, *Colonial Williamsburg* (New York: Harry Abrams, 1986), cover text.

16. Richard Handler and Eric Gable, *The New History in an Old Museum: Creating the Past at Colonial Williamsburg* (Durham, NC: Duke University Press, 1997), 6–7.

17. Ibid., 205.

18. Tity DeVries, "Ambiguity in an Alaskan Theme Park: Presenting 'History as Commodity' and 'History as Heritage,'" *Public Historian* 29, no. 2 (Spring 2007): 56.

19. "Notes from Conner Prairie Advisory Meeting," September 8, 1964, CP Archive.

20. Elizabeth Kryder-Reid, "Sites of Power and the Power of Sight: Vision in the California Mission Landscapes," in *Sites Unseen: Landscape and Vision* ed. Dianne Harris and D. Fairchild Ruggles (Pittsburgh, PA: University of Pittsburgh Press, 2007): 181–212.

21. Patricia West, *Domesticating History: The Political Origins of America's House Museums* (Washington, DC: Smithsonian Institution Press, 1999), 97.

22. Madison, *Eli Lilly*, 172.

23. Numerous studies have shown that the public views museums as inherently trustworthy. One example is from the Reach Advisors blog at http://reachadvisors.typepad.com titled "The Magic of Seven-Year-Olds," August 7, 2009.

24. Michael Wallace, *Mickey Mouse History and Other Essays on American Memory* (Philadelphia: Temple University Press, 1996), 10.

25. Tillman Bubenzer to Eli Lilly, January 14, 1963, CP Archive.

26. "Conner Prairie Advisory Committee Meeting Minutes," September 4, 1968, CP Archive.

27. Ibid.

28. Ibid.

29. "Earlham Board Meeting Minutes," June 30, 1969, CP Archive.

30. "Landrum Bolling to Guy Jones," May 23, 1969, CP Archive.

31. Evidence of a Native American village site has been located at the northern edge of Conner Prairie's property. Just twenty miles north of Conner Prairie is the Strawtown-Koteewi archaeological site. Researchers at this dig site have uncovered extensive evidence of precontact Native American habitation that dates to circa 1200 CE.

32. Diane Barthel-Bouchier, *Cultural Heritage and the Challenge of Sustainability* (Walnut Creek, CA: Left Coast Press, 2013), 138.

33. "Hog Farm Grosses $250,000," *The Farm* (Winter 1956), 53.

34. Myron Vourax, interview with Timothy Crumrin, August 31, 2004, transcript, CP Archive, 7.

35. Myron Vourax, "The Conner Prairie Concept," 1975, presented at the Association for Living History, Farm and Agricultural Museums Annual Meeting, CP Archive, 4.

36. Ibid., 2.

37. "Dedication Ceremonies [for the] Pioneer Village," March 31, 1974, CP Archive.

38. Ibid.

39. John Schippers, "History of Village and Village Construction," November 1996, CP Archive.

40. Stacy Roth, *Past into Present: Effective Techniques for First-Person Historical Interpretation* (Chapel Hill: University of North Carolina Press, 1998), 31.

41. Ibid., 32.

4

EXAMINING SUCCESSFUL FIRST-PERSON INTERPRETATION

William Faulkner famously described the presence of the past in everyday life in his novel *Requiem for a Nun* (1951): "The past is never dead. It's not even past."[1] Noted travel author William Least Heat-Moon took a page from Faulkner: "People who think the past lives on in Sturbridge Village or Mystic Seaport haven't seen Fredricksburg [Texas]. Things live on here in the only way the past ever lives—by not dying."[2]

The best preservation of a historic time period often arises from neglect. Towns off the beaten path, buildings maintained but never updated, and ephemera moldering under a layer of dust in a forgotten trunk become the prized historic treasures of the postmodern age. Are recreations of the past at museums truly living history? Are we not merely creating a stage and performing interpretations of the past? What if we have no stage or the stage is incongruous with the time period we intend to portray?

Museums around the country without historic structures have employed first-person interaction as a technique to engage people. This chapter will explore a few case studies from museums that are not traditionally considered to be part of the living history genre—a science museum, a natural history museum, a history center, and a children's museum.

Living history can happen outside of an ostensibly historic context. It has done so for years at history museums with indoor exhibits that use staged interactions with costumed characters as a technique for engaging the public. Other types of museums have also experimented with what they variously call "enactment," "living history," and "first-person interpretation." A detailed dive into both museum theater and common museum terminology around interpretive styles can be found in Tessa Bridal's 2013 book *Effective Exhibit Interpretation and Design*.[3] The following sections contain interviews and dialogue between the author and practitioners and managers who use costumed interpretation to promote learning in their museum.

THE POWER OF CHILDREN AT THE CHILDREN'S MUSEUM OF INDIANAPOLIS

In 2007, The Children's Museum of Indianapolis (hereafter referred to as TCM) opened a new gallery focused on the stories of how three remarkable children responded with courage to difficult situations. The program team for *The Power of Children* exhibit chose to use first-person characterizations to bring to life the stories of Ruby Bridges, Ryan White, and Anne Frank. Since its inception, *The Power of Children* has been lauded as both a great example of how to promote meaningful civic discourse in a children's museum and as having an exceedingly well-executed series of first-person stage shows.[4]

Notably, *The Power of Children* was developed by a team with skills and background in theater and then TCM hired trained actors to perform the first-person scripted vignettes as either the historical figure themselves or as a historical person who knew Ryan White, Ruby Bridges, or Anne Frank well. The following is a transcription of a dialogue between the author and Rachael Mathews and John Goodson of TCM.

David Allison (hereafter referred to as DA): Describe the development process for *The Power of Children*. How did the team strike upon the idea of using first-person characterizations? Were there any examples at TCM where you used first-person characters prior to *The Power of Children*?

Rachael Mathews and John Goodson (hereafter referred to as RM and JG): Prior to the opening of *The Power of Children (POC)* gallery, TCM had explored using museum theater and first-person characters, but not on quite the same level and with the same purposefulness and

Figure 4.1.   An actor at The Children's Museum of Indianapolis portrays Anne Frank at *The Power of Children* exhibit. Source: Photo courtesy of The Children's Museum of Indianapolis.

focus. Our director of interpretation at the time, Tessa Bridal, was really a driving force behind the push to utilize live first-person accounts in the gallery. She quite literally wrote the book on museum theater. We had seen previous success in first-person museum theater and wanted to harness that great potential for emotionally viable and sensitive experiential family learning moments. It is much easier to talk about these very heavy and complicated issues by first engaging the heart and connecting with a personal story.

The idea for *POC* came from a few different places:

- Jeanne White-Ginder, Ryan White's mother, contacted us upon her decision to move to Florida, asking if we wanted the contents of Ryan's bedroom.

- We had hosted a traveling exhibition similar to Anne Frank's story in (at that time) the recent past called *David's Story* that was highly successful.
- We had begun something called the POCA awards—a project headed by our volunteer department, which highlighted extraordinary youth social service projects in the greater Indianapolis area.
- I believe Ruby's story came a little bit later, but I cannot fully recall, and will need to investigate to find out exactly where she came into the timeline.

The first-person performances were an original part of the design, driven by our CEO and executed by Tessa Bridal. The idea was to connect these stories to the visitors through dramatic representation, with the goal of afterward facilitating a more in-depth discussion and unpacking of emotional and social consequences of these stories as well as the larger humanitarian piece (children have the power to make a difference—children like you).

We had been doing first-person performances throughout the building prior to this, but these were definitely new territory in terms of having a closed off, dedicated space, the subject matter (which included relevant social issues), and a postshow discussion with audience. Some examples of prior programs were Rosie the Riveter in the *Norman Rockwell* exhibit, Mary Anning in *Dinosphere*, Lilly Theater productions (full children's theater plays), and formal programming in exhibits as characters such as Ms. Frizzle in the *Magic School Bus* exhibit.

DA: What do you call what your actors do (first-person interpretation, enacting, something else?) and what do you call your actors (enactors, interpreters, actors, something else)? Why did you make those choices?

RM and JG: We call our team of full-time actors "actor interpreters" ("AIs" for short) or sometimes just "actors." We refer to the pieces themselves in a little bit of a wider vocabulary though. Part of the challenge is to represent the experience accurately for the guests in language that is clear and understandable for the widest range of people. We may say "live performance," "live theater performance," "actor performance," "immersive experience," or sometimes even "hear the story of/about." It also depends on the type of museum theater piece we are doing. Some pieces are very standard theater like in *POC* where you sit in a room, we close the doors, dim the lights, and do a performance. Some are more immersive and experiential like in our *Take Me There: China* exhibit where we ask the audience to play a part or join us in a theatrical moment onstage. Some pieces are large-scale pieces in the atrium and some are informal pieces with a costumed actor.

DA: What kinds of evaluation do you do on the program?

RM and JG: Every program we write, whether theatrical or educational, has clear goals, objectives, expected family learning outcomes, and strategies for success. When we train, rehearse, and plan, we do so with an eye for achieving those goals. When we evaluate we are looking to see that what we planned for is happening and things that aren't as well. This information reinforces our work or informs adjustments, retraining, rewriting, or adjusting expectations. When it comes to the theatrical pieces it can be a little more challenging since a lot of what we are hoping to accomplish is emotional and not always the easiest to assess and evaluate. I can hear if someone asks or answers an open-ended question, but I might not be able to tell if they felt moved by a piece. The way we try to gauge those outcomes is through postshow discussions. Ideally, in the case of *POC*, I really believe that the pieces are a tool for the conversation but the ultimate goal is to engage in a dialogue about the gallery content. Harnessing the empathy created during the performance makes for a powerful discussion afterward.

We often do different types of evaluation, which will require different tools. As the director of the pieces, I am looking for not only an extraordinary acting performance but an extraordinary discussion. I will use a more standard theater performance evaluation sheet for the piece (notes on diction, beats and transitions, character's physical/emotional life, build, audience connection, etc.). Then we will use a second evaluation form that looks at the piece objectively to see if the piece is hitting its programmatic goals. Usually, since it is a memorized piece and the program has been deemed to meet those expectations, we almost always hit the mark.

We also have begun trying to assess the quality of the postshow discussions to better determine how best to train staff to facilitate those conversations. Asking the right questions in the right order can lead to a very powerful discussion. However, asking an awkward question or [asking] in a confusing order will lead to a stilted or completely ineffective discussion. It has been a very interesting learning process, especially as we developed the live theater performances for our newest exhibit—*Sacred Journeys*. The pieces are meant to be informal first-person accounts of a powerful journey taken to answer some of life's big questions. We developed two goals—one for the piece and one specifically for the postshow discussion. The goal was to get guests to reflect on an experience in their lives. The challenge has been in how to frame that discussion and how to transition the audience's role from a "receiver" to a "participator."

DA: How do you plan for and design new programs?

RM and JG: Currently, we plan programming using a basic outline of Goal, Objectives, and Strategies for Success—all of which are attached to the exhibit Big Idea. Then we build in a plan for Family Learning Behaviors, which is the heart of our mission (Family Learning). Here, we pick from a set of researched behaviors that we find will work with the design of the program with the goal of families displaying these behaviors as a sign of family learning (working together, sharing memories, investigating for answers, etc.). Staff are trained with all of these outlined from the beginning.

Once a program has been on the floor through a remedial phase, we go out and observe for those objectives, strategies, and Family Learning behaviors in order to determine if we are meeting our planned goals at the rate we set (we set metrics for these during the planning phase and we compare back with our departmental standards).

DA: What are some of the most common responses from adults to the shows?

RM and JG: As might be imagined, there are usually very emotional responses to the pieces. I think, in general, most guests are not expecting the level of emotional work that they are about to experience. We try to prepare them with a curtain speech and set the correct mood, but ultimately it will come down to their willingness to "go there" with us. Many times, the adults will be answering questions for their children or explaining complicated topics for them. Occasionally, we have parents who choose to disengage and either play on their phones or stay in the back of the room, but that is not as common as the engaged adult. They often have questions of their own or are willing to share a specific memory or experience that relates to the story. Other common responses are on how we create and prepare the pieces themselves since they are very truthful and immersive. Depending on the story, their responses may come from a more personal place than a more knowledge recall place. We try to harness both ends of that spectrum because ultimately, if we can make the knowledge personal, we have captured both the logic and emotions portions of the gallery's goals. The fact that the stories are almost always told from a first-person perspective allows guests to connect in a personal way as well.

We have an outline that we have our staff use to create a postshow that fits a pattern of inquiry and reflection specific to the show and subject matter. Oftentimes, visitors ask basic questions about the child or story/time period, and then at times will move into the why would/how could questions, and end on a note of empowering children and families to explore ways they can make a positive different around them.

DA: How do kids respond to the show (allowing for variation by age group)?

RM and JG: Kids in general are more willing and receptive to the story and the postshow discussion. They may not be as outwardly emotionally responsive, but they most definitely "get it." They pick on the unfairness, the cruelty, the fear, and sadness, and are able to vocalize their understanding. They typically ask really good questions, not just about details of the story, but also bigger concepts of motivations for people's actions or why something happened. The more substantial answers tend to come from the eight- to twelve-year-olds, which is our target audience for the pieces anyway. The younger audiences may not fully grasp some of the story points and may be more confused by some of the subject matter, but we typically try to scaffold down our questions and try our best to make the story and the discussion accessible for the younger audiences. School groups tend to have really solid postshow discussions and that may be in part due to the fact that they are prepared and primed for a learning experience and they know that they have to respond. Regardless, they are able to articulate great observations and make great connections to their lives and the world around them.

The responses have been overwhelmingly positive when talking about kids in the range of comprehension. It's interesting to hear questions from kids about topics like racism and hatred—they are often confused and perplexed by the behavior or people committing these acts. At the same time, though, they often demonstrate a really beautiful level of insight and positivity. It's pretty cool to witness.

DA: What do you see as the value of first-person characterization in *The Power of Children* for TCM and your audience?

RM and JG: I always reflect on the times when we have Ryan White's mother here to speak in the *POC* gallery and how powerful it is and how easy it is to forget that the items in the cases with the beautifully typed labels all belonged to a real person who has a real story. In an attempt to replicate that experience in a theatrical sense, I am always hoping to harness that personal connection. In another respect, if we only looked at these stories as Jews experienced this . . . people with AIDS experience this . . . and African Americans experienced this . . . then we are already losing the battle for the conversation. When we start talking about people as a group instead of individuals, we stop seeing them as people. If we can make the story about a person, then we can suddenly transfer that potential experience of one person to the larger group experience. You can truly humanize the story. We are a storytelling people, and we crave that story. Even our weather reports are stories with protagonists and antagonists and a climax, we even name our hurricanes. We humanize our history by telling a personal account.

We modeled this idea in our writing of the stories for our *Sacred Journeys* first-person actor stories as well and have seen them used in a nonhistorical realm as well. No matter how many millions of pilgrims take journeys to sacred places, it will always boil down to a personal experience. By telling a personal story, we have specific emotional moments to connect to as an audience. Those connections are what make us care, and that would not be as possible without the potential of a first-person experience.

These stories are easy to separate yourself from emotionally—events that happened in the past, and therefore not something to think too hard about in relation to one's current life. However, when they are told in this way, the stories come to life and visitors connect with them on an emotional level that just does not happen in the gallery itself. Theater is such a powerful tool for stimulating an emotional response, and we've seen evidence of it time and time again—of the success that this type of programming can achieve.

HISTORY PLAYERS AT THE MINNESOTA HISTORY CENTER

When I spoke with staff at the Minnesota History Center (hereafter referred to as MHC), this state-run historical society was in a time of transition with their first-person interpretive program. In 2015 and 2016, History Players—MHC's umbrella name for their costumed programming—went through a "sunsetting" process, due primarily to the high costs of staffing and supporting it. MHC's History Players program had been a keystone offering for a multiplicity of audiences since 1992, and I was curious about how the program was perceived by the public and how it morphed throughout its lifespan.

I sat down with Jack Matheson, Suzanne de la Houssaye, Laurie R. Johnson, Katie McKee, Mary Mannes, and Daryl Jorgenson on December 8, 2015, on a rainy day in St. Paul at the MHC. Each of these MHC staff members both performed as a History Player and held a number of other administrative and educational roles within the organization.

David Allison (hereafter referred to as DA): What does first-person interaction provide for your audience?

Laurie R. Johnson (hereafter referred to as LJ): Living history fulfills our mission statement to a tee by making a deep connection to transform lives. It transforms our lives as well as the people we are with. We are planting historical seeds that grow and then they internalize and then remember that experience and come back. It is such a tangible connection with the community. It is the difference between online dating and actual dating.

Suzanne de la Houssaye (hereafter referred to as SH): Seniors in particular connect with the characters. It is an interpersonal connection—they make connections in a way that is really profound. It is like we were their friends. Over the course of a fifty-minute experience, they can make connections with us as the characters.

Katie McKee (hereafter referred to as KM): With the History Players, at least momentarily, there is a suspension of disbelief—they think you have experienced those things, and they can see how historical figures could have done that. Visitors believe the character is a real person—that I am who that person was.

DA: How do kids respond to costumed characters?

Daryl Jorgenson (hereafter referred to as DJ): We like to give the class an experience that they won't get from a textbook or a sign—there is a reality and physicality to an object or story that we can provide them with through History Players.

Jack Matheson (hereafter referred to as JM): You create a safe space in your presentation and you inherently include them in that space—they can ask questions they haven't thought of before. As the keeper of a safe space, you have an opportunity to provoke questions.

DA: What about other audiences? How did History Players address the needs of adult audiences?

KM: Thomas Lyles was an African American activist and entrepreneur. When our performer would go out and speak to senior women in greater Minnesota using his first-person character of Thomas Lyles, he was able to more deftly address racism and got to the core of the human experience to have those conversations. Costumed characters bridge the divide—there is always something in the story that they can relate to. This sort of dialogue is what our society needs. Important conversations can happen in that setting.

Mary Mannes (hereafter referred to as MM): There is always a sense of play involved. You can use humor to get them hooked in. The program becomes a dialogue where you listen to answers from the audience and then incorporate it into the response. You can come back to those questions—it is a skill that can come out through the performance.

SH: We provided dress-up opportunities for the kids and adults—everyone loves to role play. In one of our programs, a boy and a girl come up and pretend to be two well-to-do Minnesotans and act out the jostling of the carriage, and it's really history gold.

JM: For all audiences, the material culture can become an end point to the conversation, and the audience then becomes a part of the performance as a result of the artifacts.

LJ: You can connect both emotionally and with the senses through the conversations you can have with people—it can be a hugely powerful experience.

DA: Can you describe some of the challenges of your History Players program that led to it being discontinued this year?

KM: The program was growing, but we didn't have a solid business plan. We went after the grants rather than looking at the overall health of the program. Ultimately, the biggest challenge was that sending someone out to schools was really costly. They would perform only one performance and then have to travel back. It was lots of driving. When you're working with schools, finding the right pricing model is key.

DA: How might you incorporate some of the learnings from your experiences with first-person narratives into programming at MHC in the future?

MM: We do think that outreach programs in the future will have first-person narratives as a key part of them.

JM: History Players is the foundation of the videoconferencing programming that we launched recently. Thirty percent of our programs are booked outside of the state. The strengths of the History Players program inform all of the programming we provide digitally.

LJ: When I teach classes for kids we try to take them back in time and help them to learn something intimate about history. It is useful in teaching those classes. The skills we gained through History Players transfer to interacting with all audiences in all settings.

After our interview, the staff at MHC generously provided me with some documents from the early days of first-person interpretation at the history center. Something I noted very quickly that separates MHC from other, more didactic living history portrayals was their deliberate acknowledgment that interacting with costumed characters is a strange experience. A training document from circa 1992, titled "First Impression: Introducing Your History Player Character to the Public" by Wendy Ellefson, outlines the pitfalls of poor first-person interpretation. After laying out a nightmare scenario in which an unwilling visitor is subjected to the onslaught of an overzealous "bizarre creature draped in layers and layers of lace and crinoline, flecked with sparkling beads and crowned in ringlets and feathers" who foists herself on a visitor who "may only be thinking about lunch," Ellefson describes how living history "need(s) to be approached with a great sensitivity to its inherent difficulties."[5]

The document then continues by exploring some of the differences between living history museums and first-person characterizations in museums: "The advantage to working in a living history museum is that you have the support of the appropriate sensory stimuli to give your character its *raison d'etre*."[6] Ellefson then mentions that the public expects the strangeness of a first-person character at living history museums and contrasts that expectation with the situation in a traditional museum exhibit: "Unfortunately, indoor museum curators are not too keen about slopping around a little animal fat and sawdust or stoking up a roaring fire for the sake of your living history verisimilitude. . . . You may need to work twice as hard to overcome your character's incongruity and ease the visitor into your interpretation."[7]

Ellefson then expounds upon the advantages of museum-bounded living history: "Because your character is obviously out of its element and you acknowledge that fact in your interpretation, you are free to comment on an infinite number of topics. You can easily compare your character's life to the visitor's life and offer insights that you might not be able to provide if you were bound to a specific, recreated 'time' and 'place.'"[8] These advantages transcend history museums, and the next case study will showcase how a natural history museum uses first-person interpretation to illuminate the stories it tells.

ENACTORS AT THE DENVER MUSEUM OF NATURE AND SCIENCE

Natural history museums and science centers rarely use costumed historical enactors as a part of their interpretive repertoire. Indeed, when the Denver Museum of Nature and Science (hereafter referred to as DMNS) started its enactor program in 2007, the program coordinators had to look to history museums for their inspiration. That year DMNS hosted a temporary exhibit titled *Benjamin Franklin: In Search of a Better World*. As is often the case with temporary exhibits brought in from outside the museum, DMNS decided to enhance the exhibit to add more interest for their guests—this time through the use of historical enactors to portray composite characters who knew Benjamin Franklin.

Kathleen Tinworth, an in-house researcher who conducted an in-depth study about the enactment program, wrote that "the program was striving for an interaction which put the visitors on an equal footing with the characters, allowing for conversation and a greater chance of personal relevance for the visitor."[9] The enactors' success, as evidenced by a plethora of platitudes from visitors, led to DMNS deciding to continue the program for another historically based temporary exhibit. Shortly after *Benjamin Franklin*, DMNS hosted *Titanic: The Artifact Exhibition*, which ran from 2007 to 2008. For *Titanic*, DMNS expanded the enactor program to include scripted vignettes in addition to the standard interactive techniques commonly used by first-person costumed interpreters.

Since *Benjamin Franklin* and *Titanic*, DMNS has used historical enactors in four other temporary exhibits—*Real Pirates*, *A Day in Pompeii*, *Traveling the Silk Road*, and, in 2015 and 2016, *The International Exhibi-*

tion of Sherlock Holmes. Two people were constants from *Benjamin Franklin* in 2007 up through *Sherlock Holmes* in 2015—Jennifer Moss Logan, the coordinator for the enactor program, and Michael Parker, an enactor and a senior educator/performer on the DMNS team. Michael has portrayed a character (or multiple characters) in each of these exhibits, and Jennifer has recruited, hired, supervised, and led the team while also serving as a strong advocate for the program. As the temporary exhibit enactor program has grown, so too has a burgeoning ongoing presence for enactors in DMNS' diorama halls and permanent exhibit galleries.

Below are excerpts from an interview with Jennifer Moss-Logan and Michael Parker conducted by the author on July 29, 2015.

David Allison (hereafter assigned initials DA): What distinguishes enacting from other types of interpretation?

Figure 4.2.   Denver Museum of Nature and Science enactors José Zuniga and Isaiah Kelly interact with a guest in the *Traveling the Silk Road* temporary exhibit in 2015. Source: © Denver Museum of Nature and Science.

Michael Parker (hereafter assigned initials MP): An enactor doesn't have a context to fall back on [like in living history museums]. We have to do different work to get people into the moment. We teach the audience their role—I use something to link them to the time, like showing off my pocket watch or asking them if they came to the museum via a carriage. It's always helpful to ask visitors questions that are easy to answer and emotionally driven. A series of small rhetorical questions can get them comfortable talking to you.

Jennifer Moss-Logan (hereafter assigned initials JML): Enactment in the museum setting blends authenticity with casualness in a way that is different from other types of interpretation. There is a place in museums for all types of interpretation because there are many types of visitors. But we've found that with first-person enactment, visitors connect in a personal way to the topic at hand that is different from a third-person style. For example, with the *Titanic* exhibit, third-person facilitators can bring boarding passes to visitors' attention and talk about them. But if a passenger on the *Titanic* introduces themselves, then the visitor can develop empathy with people from a past time in a richer way.

It also provides a different kind of context to objects—the relevancy and personal connection is so rich. Visitors remember it and go home and tell people about it. Interaction with a character is accessible and different than what you might normally expect to find at a museum.

DA: Do you ever have moments when the line between the character you are playing and yourself as Michael Parker blur?

MP: My wife will sometimes say to me after I've been enacting all day, "You know that you're not actually a newspaper reporter." I really do become that person for seven or eight hours. I like to create a character that has a backstory similar to my own life experiences. Doing this [job] is as cathartic to the enactor as it is to the guest.

DA: Tell me more about why enacting has been valued by DMNS since you started the program in 2007.

MP: From the beginning of time, storytelling has been how we connect with each other. Relating to one another as human beings happens best through stories. Enacting provides great opportunities to tell unique stories every day.

JML: It allows us to tackle difficult issues in a more graceful way. When a character who is, for example, against women's suffrage says, "I feel like this . . . ," it is substantially different than if they were to read a text panel on a wall describing the controversy of the time period. I think that visitors are able to think more deeply and critically when they hear it from an actual person instead of the detachment of the text on a label.

MP: People come back to see us. We have fans! I think that enactors just make the experience more interesting, accessible, and fun. The content is not staid, and it's different than just going to an exhibit and walking through. It provides a spark for conversations within families and groups.

JML: In a study done [Kathleen Tinworth's 2008 evaluation], people who were called six weeks later about their experience at the museum were most likely to talk about the enactors. It is also a program that is flexible to other types of experiences—we have used them for our Distance Learning program and our Field Trip Adventures, as well as special events and fundraisers. The program is really flexible and provides endless opportunities to spark curiosity.

While the energy of DMNS' enactor program has gained traction with the museum's audience in the past few years, a science center has been using theatrical techniques for as long as most living history museums have used first-person characterizations. Most museum professionals point to the Science Museum of Minnesota (hereafter referred to as SMM) as the granddaddy of live theater interpretation in science museums. They have had a vigorous museum theater program since the mid-1970s. Next is an interview with Stephanie Long, Michael Ritchie, and Melanie Wehrmacher from SMM. Michael and Melanie are performers and Stephanie is the theater program's director.

THEATER AND EXHIBIT ACTORS AT THE SCIENCE MUSEUM OF MINNESOTA

David Allison (hereafter referred to as DA): How did SMM strike upon the idea of live theater?

Stephanie Long (hereafter referred to as SL): One of the museum's security guards actually wrote the first play in the 1970s. We consider ourselves to have the longest-running professional theater company in a museum. By "professional" I mean that they have four years of training or the equivalent before getting the job.

DA: When did first-person characterizations start for you?

SL: It would have been 2007 with the *Titanic* exhibit. We had actors portraying actual stewards and staff members on the *Titanic*. We developed a training model that we still use—twenty hours of research into content and background information and then twenty hours of rehearsals. We always have a dialect coach for them. We've also developed character background worksheets and quiz shows during training so they can build their knowledge of the time period and their biographies.

DA: What makes the first-person characterizations you do at the museum unique?

SL: The performers really have to be so multitalented. They put the research that they've done into action through conversations with the audience. Their repertoire of shows is large, and they have to be able to memorize those shows and then not be scheduled to do it, but then pick it back up after a few weeks.

DA: First-person interpretation really is a specialized skill set, isn't it?

SL: Yes, it is. They have to be able to have facts at their disposal but also be flexible by using their social intelligence to answer questions and then use different techniques depending on the situation.

DA: How do you most often make connections with your audience when you are portraying a character?

Melanie Wehrmacher (hereafter referred to as MW): It is always a balancing act of fun and additional information. We have to make it clear that we have something for them that will be interesting. Some people have a terror of interacting with people in costume. It is always good to have an "in"—a subject like food and clothing can work every time with the audience.

Michael Ritchie (hereafter referred to as MR): In every exhibit—no matter the content focus—things that we still do today make connections to people.

DA: What are some advantages of live interpretation over exhibits or other educational settings?

MW: It's free choice learning. I can't tell you the number of times someone has come up after a show and said, "If only my science teacher were like this, I would have loved this stuff."

SL: In a recent evaluation, 97 percent of respondents picked shows as their favorite or second favorite part of the experience at the museum.

MR: Visitors just don't get as much out of their experience or enjoy it as much if they don't see a show or interact with a character.

SL: It is all about the group joy and social fun that visitors can have with us. When kids from a school group squeal in delight in unison at the demonstrations, you know the interaction is working.

From these interviews from TCM, Conner Prairie, MHC, and SMM, it is clear that the heritage from the 1970s approach to living history is alive and kicking. Let's explore the antecedents to the modern iterations of living history by taking a look at how Conner Prairie conceptualized living history in the 1970s as Prairietown was built.

LIVING HISTORY PHILOSOPHY IN THE 1970S

Folklorist Henry Glassie believed that Prairietown at Conner Prairie was an "affirmation of the regular people who have been on the Indiana frontier."[10] Myron Vourax, Conner Prairie's director in the mid-1970s, wrote that:

> Conner Prairie will educate by correcting false stereotypes about pioneer existence. For example, we assume everyone on the frontier was equal—everyone lived in log cabins which looked similar, everyone had thirty dollars, went to church and had a long rifle. The myth of the frontier tells us that rich people were just "lucky" and worked much harder than the poor people—when in fact, wealthy people came to the frontier with their wealth . . . and built huge fancy homes in the wilderness on the next farm to poor settlers in small log cabins. In reality—at Conner Prairie—the accurate past is presented. . . . The building of big, fancy houses was *simultaneous* with the building of small cabins. *That* is interesting; and *that* is *educational*. (Emphasis in original)[11]

This statement shows that Vourax and Glassie wanted to use Prairietown as a way to combat misconceptions about pioneers perpetuated by textbooks and other museums (that rich people worked harder than poor people and that everyone was equal) and to do so in a way that would be more interesting and educational to people than the myths they were attempting to bust.[12]

Conner Prairie did not have the kind of baggage of trying to interpret the stories of famous historical figures that weighed down Colonial Williamsburg, Greenfield Village, and countless plantation museums throughout the South. Because of this, Vourax and Glassie cast pioneer Indiana not only as a place of variety in social situations (as typified by the contrast between William Conner's large, two-story brick house and the small, one-story log cabins littered along the main road through Prairietown), but also as a place where you could see yourself, no matter your socioeconomic situation, in history. Another Conner Prairie director, even before Glassie and Vourax, wrote that Prairietown was being used to "demonstrate how the 'pioneer' lived, worked and played. It is not our intent to show just the wealthy and their acquisitions, nor do we wish to depict just the crude beginnings. We would like to show the average man—his struggles, his triumphs, and his growth. This is our real heritage."[13]

The average white Hoosier visitors to Conner Prairie, even if they could not identify with the types of history being told by the children (and grandchildren) of immigrants, blacks, and women who began writing history about people like themselves during this time, would most likely have placed importance on the unique Indiana stories of average people like themselves told at Prairietown. Since the East Coast was the nexus of bicentennial celebrations, perhaps some of Prairietown's popularity can also be ascribed to Hoosiers seeking to validate their forebears' efforts in the Midwest in the face of the hoopla around Lexington, Mt. Vernon, Williamsburg, and other historically significant eighteenth-century sites.

Prairietown, at the time of its dedication in 1974, was created to be a microcosm of the 1830s that told the stories of average Hoosiers. Myron Vourax and Henry Glassie had established an intellectual framework that placed Prairietown's educational focus under the aegis of entertainment. Like Conner Prairie, Plimoth Plantation and Colonial Williamsburg began moving toward first-person interpretation and an integration of social history. At this early stage, Conner Prairie's unique stories of pioneer life focused on entertainment as a means to educate.

NOTES

1. William Faulkner, *Requiem for a Nun* (New York: Random House, 1951).
2. William Least Heat-Moon, *Blue Highways: A Journey into America* (New York: Little, Brown and Company, 1982), 144.
3. Tessa Bridal, *Effective Exhibit Interpretation and Design* (Lanham, MD: AltaMira Press, 2013).
4. Elizabeth Wood and Sarah Cole, "Can You Do That in a Children's Museum?" *Museum and Social Issues* 2, no. 2 (Fall 2007): 193–200.
5. Wendy Ellefson, "First Impressions: Introducing Your History Player Character to the Public," Minnesota History Center, circa 2012, 1.
6. Ibid., 2.
7. Ibid., 2.
8. Ibid., 3.
9. Kathleen Tinworth, "2007 Enactor Program Evaluation: A Summary of Quantitation and Qualitative Results," Denver Museum of Nature and Science, 2008.
10. Henry Glassie, interview by Timothy Crumrin, May 27, 2005, transcript, CP Archive, 13.
11. Myron Vourax, "Underlying Philosophy and Tour Plan of Conner Prairie Pioneer Settlement in Accordance with Dr. Henry Glassie, Chief Consultant," March 14, 1975, CP Archive.

12. Although there is no direct evidence to show that Eli Lilly agreed with this perspective, in *Eli Lilly: A Life, 1885–1977* (Indianapolis: Indiana Historical Society Press, 2006), James Madison intimates that Lilly's frequent visits and generous financial backing to Conner Prairie was tacit approval of the type of history being portrayed at Conner Prairie during this time.

13. Harold Cope, "Director's Statement to Joint Meeting of the Conner Prairie Advisory Council and the Earlham Board of Trustees," April 18, 1970, Earlham College Archive.

5

OPENING DOORS AT CONNER PRAIRIE

In chapter 4, we explored examples of living history and first-person characterization from the Denver Museum of Nature and Science, the Science Museum of Minnesota, the Minnesota History Center, and The Children's Museum of Indianapolis and got a glimpse into the philosophical basis for Prairietown at Conner Prairie. In this chapter we will return in greater depth to Conner Prairie as our central case study for how living history has transformed over time. An important caveat here is that the antecedents for living history—pageants and costumed house tours—are not explored herein, but the literature about both historical pageants of the 1920s and 1930s and traditional historic house tours is both broad and deep. These merit the more extensive histories that have been written about them elsewhere and are fascinating in their own right. To frame our conversation about engagement at Conner Prairie, the meat of this chapter is preceded by a short personal incident from the frontlines of living history.

STORY FROM THE FRONTLINES OF LIVING HISTORY

I hadn't been in my new position as agricultural specialist for long before I found myself at the reins of a team of massive Percheron horses. Having gotten the knack of harnessing these two lovely black mares, I was filled with confidence for my first solo outing with Rose and Belle. These two were Conner Prairie's draft horses, who ended up bearing the brunt of the work for the occasional wagon rides for visitors and the wild gallops across the covered bridge during October's "Headless Horseman" fall public program. Rose was "moon blind" in her left eye, and she was the more skittish of the two as a result. Belle was friendly but demanding in a typically equine way—horses are the cats of the domesticated barnyard critter world. Cattle are most analogous to dogs, which is why I always gravitated to the amiable dopiness of our bovine herd.

But I was confident in my newfound skills with horses and ready to put myself to the test. Jeff, the senior agriculture specialist, had helped me hitch up a 1880s-era manure spreader to the harness. The manure spreader had a wicked set of exposed tines for churning the poop out the back of the wagon, and its massive metal wheels had deep grooves and ridges. I sat up on the wooden bench behind Rose and Belle and waited for Jeff to tell me what to do.

He encouraged me to drive the spreader around the new 1886 farmhouse—which was only a couple months shy of being completed—and then pull around to the field crisscrossed with corn stubble to get started on our smelly task. I cavalierly asked the horses to "get up" and then tried to maintain a firm yet fluid grip on the leather reins.

In my enthusiasm to prove myself, I had neglected to clarify Jeff's request to drive around the farmhouse, and instead of taking the dirt path on the outside of the picket fence, I drove the mares straight up the red brick walkway that encircled the porch. Rose and Belle could sense my rising panic as I realized that I wouldn't have enough room to squeeze the spreader between the fence and the side of the porch in front of the house. They snuffled and pawed the ground as I "whoa-ed" them and considered my options. Perhaps unsurprisingly, I chose the worst option—I decided to proceed through the narrow gap. The horses smoothly stepped through the space between the porch and the fence and, fully of their own canny volition, made the turn to get back onto the dirt path.

The manure spreader didn't fare so well, though, and I heard a chunk of the wooden porch crack ominously as Rose and Belle leaned against the harness to yank the machine past the obstacle behind them. The perturbed project manager and construction supervisor for the farmhouse emerged from the front door with a look of incredulity on his face as I jumped down from the spreader and lamely tried to place the piece of the porch back where it belonged. Not only had I ruined a newly installed and painted porch, but the wheels of the spreader had cut deep ruts into the damp spring front lawn, which had been freshly planted with grass seed not a week earlier.

Had I been raised on a farm like the folks who originally used that manure spreader, I would never have made such a rookie mistake. As a lifelong city dweller, my range of experience was thoroughly estranged from the useful knowledge that would have been secondhand for the rural farmhands of the past. How do first-person interpreters bridge the gap between the past and present, and how did that gap become filled in with minutia rather than compelling stories? This next section will explore this conundrum.

ENGAGEMENT ON THE WANE: 1980S AND 1990S AT CONNER PRAIRIE

The 1930s-style pageants and house tours gave way to a social history focus as Prairietown became the cornerstone of interpretive programming at Conner Prairie in the mid-1970s. In the wake of the sweeping changes as to how interpreters in Prairietown presented history to the public, as elucidated through Myron Vourax's "Conner Prairie Concept," visitor comments pointed to the attention to detail that Vourax championed. In 1975, a visitor to Prairietown said about his experience there, "I felt I had visited real people in their homes. Late that night it began to snow very hard, and I found myself wondering how those people out on the prairie were doing."[1] This empathy is precisely what Conner Prairie intended to happen through its first-person characterizations. Vourax wrote, "Conner Prairie is one of the few places where an atmosphere conducive to . . . reflection [can take place]. . . . Our first person presentation and our desire not [to] commercialize your experience . . . will, we hope, enhance your enjoyment and appreciation."[2] Despite the strangeness of the other culture of the 1830s depicted in Prairietown, interpreters were trained to make the experience as accessible to modern audiences as possible. Vourax again gave voice to this sentiment: "Our present and future success depends on how extraordinarily easy we make it for others to honor and enjoy the past."[3]

By the time of Prairietown's development in the 1970s, many people had begun to distance themselves from an authoritarian style of educational philosophy.[4] Places like Conner Prairie, which offered an integrated, hands-on approach to history, became popular field trip destinations for teachers seeking to provide experiences to their students that could not occur in the classroom. John Dewey's theory of experiential instrumentalism was becoming well entrenched in educational circles,[5] and Conner Prairie, by allowing children to see, touch, and do at the site, reflected this theoretical approach to a high degree. A 1977 article in a member magazine by Conner Prairie's curator of education, Willard Moore,[6] explained how Conner Prairie intended to appeal to teachers:

> [P]erhaps one of the most pivotal groups in the region is the school teachers and college instructors who teach our children and use the museum as a resource site for learning. Our responsibilities in this quarter are largely by-products of our educational system—democratic, inclusive and, lately, tending toward interdisciplinary programs.[7]

Conner Prairie's associate director in 1978, Robert Ronsheim, echoed and expanded on Moore's thoughts by giving a brief history of "village museums" and describing the experiences as primarily "gestalt" and "holistic."[8] Ronsheim explained that the gestalt nature of living museums provides an antidote to the fact that museums could never be totally accurate in detail.[9] That is, they could provide a greater emphasis on the processes of crafts and the lifeways of the people of the past than on the content and details of the past "as it really was."

Because it was impossible to truly recreate the past, village museums served their audiences best when they gave a sense and a feel of the past through the representation of a relatable community of fellow human beings.[10] This article by Ronsheim shows that the Skansen-style folklife museum model was still preeminent at Conner Prairie in the late 1970s. A strict adherence to educational goals had not yet become the driving force behind the presentations to the public as it did during the 1980s.

Ronsheim also realized that the ability to convey social history at Conner Prairie would be enhanced if the public had an opportunity to engage with the experience. "The distance between the present and the past can be effectively interpreted at an outdoor museum with the help of the material context . . . and by engaging the visitors—by getting the visitors to participate."[11] Participation was seen as key to helping visitors make connections to their own lives. If visitors were relegated to merely watching interpreters going about their 1836 lives, they would be much less likely to become emotionally involved with the characters or to have a physical experience that would remind them of something in their own lives and possibly lead to learning.

A collection of letters from a school group from Rushville, Indiana, who visited Prairietown in the spring of 1983, is also illustrative. Of the seven letters, three mentioned the food that the students saw being cooked. Two letters commented on the "dead animals" hanging in the houses. These types of experiences imprinted themselves in children's minds because they had a visceral physical reaction to them, as opposed to merely reading about what was cooked or about how pelts were used for trade in the 1830s. One of the letters exemplifies "scaffolding" in learning, where a student made connections between what she (or he) learned with something that she (or he) had heard about before or had already experienced. "I enjoyed coming there for our trip, because it made me think back to when my mother told me that people like you ate things like that. I didn't believe her."[12]

While the letters above show that visitors to Prairietown were enjoying the touchable, immersive spaces, staff often did not approve of how the visitors treated the environments that were created in the buildings. One anecdote from a Conner Prairie staff newspaper from July 1982 gives evidence for some of the staff's attitude toward visitors at the time. The traditional museum staffer's role as protector of artifacts figured strongly into this quote: "When you visit museums, at least the people I know . . . show some manners and discipline but I'm never sure around here. Maybe we need Plexiglas [sic] to protect us from . . . well, yesterday, a lady started tearing the bed apart to see the ropes and a man started working the loom and someone else was at the fireplace grabbing a bowl and I felt like I was going to be the next one they tore apart."[13] The type of defensiveness this interpreter expresses toward the artifacts belies best practices in learning theory, which would champion open-ended exploration and physical experiences that help make connections to visitors' lives as a way to stimulate learning.[14]

An encouragement to interpreters from management during this time highlighted the discrepancy between how many interpreters viewed their educational role and how management hoped that they would interact with the public. "A reminder to Maggies [a costumed character role] in the Conner Kitchen: as long as we are conducting school tours, you are to make bread dough for the children to knead each day. We serve bread in the dining room to begin discussing food and how it is prepared." The end goal was not to be the production of a good, edible loaf of bread for the staff's gustatory pleasure, but rather a tactile experience for the children that would lead to discussion and a more intimate understanding of the nineteenth century. The instructions continued, "Maggie is to continue the discussion and let the children participate in kneading. If you do not make bread dough, serving the finished bread in the dining room then has no importance to the tour and is merely a treat."[15]

Other similar reminders from management throughout the interpreter newsletters of the early 1980s emphasize that although management had a clear idea for how to present history in an engaging, hands-on manner, interpreters often fell back on patterns that were counterproductive to creating rich educational experiences. Many interpreters viewed the ultimate goal of their position as merely inhabiting their characters and living and working as if they were in the time period, with no effort on their part to interact with visitors or get them involved.

Institutionalization of deep characterizations with little regard to visitor experience in Prairietown in the late 1980s took the form of the creation of the Pioneer Adventure Center as an area "devoted to experiential learning and group participation for both adults and children, families as well as individuals."[16] By abdicating experiential learning to the center, Prairietown became defined by its "role-playing interpretation" that increasingly focused on lectures and content-heavy monologues from interpreters to visitors.[17] The emphasis on participatory social history that Ronsheim and Vourax had envisioned for Prairietown was losing ground.

Visitor comment cards are not typically the best way to truly gauge the effectiveness of an experience. They often highlight the very best experiences and the very worst experiences but do a poor job of giving insight into how the majority of visitors perceived their visit. The strength of comment cards, however, is that they do provide a certain measure of basic feedback on how visitors are experiencing the museum when that information is not available from more detailed studies. One theme in visitor comments from the 1980s (as tracked through their occasional appearances in the Conner Prairie internal staff newsletter) was an emphasis on the importance of first-person interpretive techniques "giving a true feeling of a pioneer village."[18] Up through the 1990s, visitors to the museum consistently returned to the experience of reliving the past and stepping back in time as the reasons why they came to Prairietown. Just as teachers did, the general public viewed the museum primarily as a place to have a tactile, visceral experience of the past and not primarily as a place to learn about history.[19]

In 1992, then Conner Prairie director Polly Jontz[20] hired an Indianapolis-based marketing and research firm to conduct an in-depth visitor learning study to discover demographic trends, to get a baseline for a typical trip to Conner Prairie, and to evaluate the competitive environment of not-for-profit organizations in central Indiana.[21] One key finding was that visitors consistently ranked Conner Prairie very highly in terms of its authenticity and the opportunities it afforded to learn about history. At the same time, they gave lowest scores to the categories of "I will probably return some day" and "It has lots of things to see and do."[22] Visitors viewed Conner Prairie as an authentic, but not terribly repeatable, attraction. Conner Prairie had devoted many resources to making Prairietown a totally accurate and detail-rich microcosm of 1830s Indiana. In the process, management had narrowed its focus to the point that visitors considered Prairietown to be always frozen in time and unchanging. As such, there was no reason to come back, because the experience would always be the exact same. Because the rote content that each interpreter presented rarely varied (due to the insistence upon conveying specific historic information to visitors), the only reason to return to Prairietown would be to reinforce those same lessons, as if the interpreters were "living exhibit panels" or tape recorders.

A long-range planning data report filed by visitor researcher Marilyn Hood in the late 1980s reminded Conner Prairie administrators (in particular Polly Jontz, who had hired Hood) about their core values from the advent of Prairietown in the 1970s. "Remember that most of your audience come [sic] for pleasure, for a good time, as well as for learning—and that combining education and entertainment offers the most satisfying experience for most visitors."[23] Hood continued with her summary of her research findings by encouraging the museum to provide "variety within consistency, flexibility within authenticity, to coax people into return visitation."[24] It was clear to Hood that visitors expected more variation from the Conner Prairie experience and would be excited by deviations from the typical Prairietown interactions with interpreters. Hood's advice was not acted upon until her findings were reinforced by another visitor study that took place as the museum continued to have faltering attendance into the late 1990s.[25]

OPENING DOORS IN THE 2000S: CONNER PRAIRIE
RETURNS TO ITS ROOTS

Throughout the 1980s, attendance figures and visitor satisfaction (as measured through surveys at Conner Prairie) had shown that merely presenting the past accurately would not be a successful way to build attendance at the museum and continue to keep the doors open.[26] By the 1990s, public history had developed to the point that learning theory, paying attention to audience needs, and using entertainment as a valid technique for piquing curiosity came into the mainstream of thought for progressive museums.[27] This audience focus hearkened back to the vision set out by Glassie and Vourax of using social history to provide an entertaining experience. It is important to note, however, that the context had changed by the 1990s (both with regard to the societal differences that arose in the intervening twenty years and with the new modes of thinking about public history), and so the seemingly same vision meant something different to administrators in the 1990s. As has been shown, staff at Conner Prairie had drawn away from Glassie's and Vourax's initial vision for Prairietown, and at the same time, were not conversant with the newer public history trends of the 1990s. It was not until a pioneering study in 1999 that the problem with living history as it was being presented at Conner Prairie (which Marilyn Hood noted in her research findings a decade earlier) was reidentified.[28]

Between 1999 and 2002, Conner Prairie conducted three separate learning studies. In all cases, researchers transcribed and analyzed the visitors' experiences at the museum. The first came about in 1999 after Ellen Rosenthal arrived at Conner Prairie to serve as vice president of operations. Having previously assisted the Pittsburgh-based Museum Learning Collaborative (MLC)[29] on studies of the Pittsburgh Children's Museum and the Heinz History Center, Rosenthal asked MLC if they would informally advise her and Conner Prairie researcher Jane Blankman-Hetrick on a study at Conner Prairie. Rosenthal's interest in finding out what visitors were learning at Conner Prairie arose from her observation of the usefulness of visitor-generated content as a contributing factor to the success of static exhibits at the Heinz History Center in Pittsburgh. She took a cue here from Michael Frisch, whose concept of "shared authority" echoed through the public history field in the 1990s.[30]

As they formulated their evaluation plan for Prairietown, Rosenthal and Blankman-Hetrick decided to limit their work to family groups and combine techniques used in various MLC studies. For the Conner Prairie study, visitors were outfitted with handheld audio recorders and video cameras. Five family groups were asked to document thirty minutes of their time at the museum with video cameras. The researchers thought that this process would provide them with an opportunity to see the Conner Prairie experience and visitor/interpreter interaction from the perspective of the visitor. However, visitors did not seem to be as interested in interacting with interpreters as they were interested in videotaping the grounds, themselves, or the other visitors who were around them. By allowing visitors to videotape their own visit, little insight was gained into how they learned, but enough information was gathered for the researchers to know that there was much to discover about visitor's experiences and that more examination was required.[31]

In the meantime, MLC conducted its own small-scale learning study at Conner Prairie in 2000. Findings from this study supported what had already been discovered in earlier studies.[32] Blankman-Hetrick and Rosenthal noted in an analysis of the results of the pilot study that "a large amount of the conversation at Prairietown was from the interpreter, not the visitor."[33] This finding was troubling to Rosenthal and John Herbst[34] as president of Conner Prairie because the dialogic approach to learning had been established as foundational to best practices in public history theory of the 1990s.

A third, full-length study was conducted in collaboration with the linguistics department at Ball State University in 2002. In order to improve the data, the researchers needed to find a way for the visitors to forget that they were being studied. They also needed a snapshot of the learning conversations that were occurring throughout the entire visit. To that end, they outfitted visitors with lapel microphones and mini-disc recorders in order to capture their entire stay at the museum. They collected fifty families' conversations resulting in over 200 hours of data that required in-depth analysis.[35]

The earlier findings were corroborated by this study, which showed few instances of interpreters and visitors actively conversing. Instead, transcripts showed multiple examples of interpretive monologues interspersed with surface-level questioning by both visitors and interpreters.

An example of "interpreter as information giver" with examples of basic questioning is the following exchange from 2002:

Interpreter: Well, you got any questions about school or anything?

Woman: I was wondering how you can afford to eat if you only make three cents a day?

Interpreter: Ma'am, I've got a farm outside of town. And you see, most of the children, a lot of them, don't even have three cents a day. So what I do is I take items to trade, see for education, so they can bring me in—you know—just like now, berries will be coming along pretty soon. So they can bring me in a pie, something like that, you know. I'll wait until next fall and say, let's see, they brought me in three pies, they brought me in a cobbler. . . . Things like that. [36]

Researchers discovered that visitors typically listened to the monologue, left the post, and, within their group, conversed with each other in an attempt to make sense of and analyze the information they had just heard. These types of interactions were problematic. With most of the learning indicators occurring after the families left the interpretive posts, questions arose that no one in the group could answer. [37] With few exceptions, interpreters did not play an active enough role in the facilitation of the learning process. This realization prompted Conner Prairie's administration to take steps toward making fundamental internal improvements. [38]

The findings from these learning studies altered how interpreters were trained. Prior to these changes, Conner Prairie's training program was content-heavy and emphasized the importance of conveying "post goals" to visitors. [39] These post goals were content-based and varied depending on the physical location the interpreter "inhabited." For example, the 1836 Prairietown innkeeper character was expected to discuss travel and transportation, women's roles, and the economy of the 1830s, regardless of whether the visitor was interested in these subjects.

In the aftermath of these learning studies, a small team of managers and interpreters from the Museum Programs Division took on the task of making significant changes to the visitor experience at Conner Prairie by redirecting the way that the interpreters conceptualized their role in visitors' learning process. By reworking the foundational training and management structures of the museum, Conner Prairie's leadership, under the direction of President John Herbst and then Vice President Ellen Rosenthal,[40] initiated a change in its organizational culture. The team's proposed changes became known as Opening Doors,[41] a reference to the new guest-focused approach that strove to "open the door" to learning. Beginning in 2003, Conner Prairie trained interpreters to provide engaging hands-on activities and a fun, interactive environment for visitors.

This new approach combined the thorough research and educational goals that are Conner Prairie's heritage with a revitalized entertainment focus that hearkened to the original intent of the museum's founders. Conner Prairie dispensed with post goals as the main focus of each post; interpreters were encouraged to try to determine what visitors were interested in by watching their body language, listening for verbal cues, and making eye contact.[42] In addition, interpreters used a variety of "hooks" to provoke visitor interest. Prior to these changes, interpreters were taught to allow visitors to look but not touch, but with the introduction of Opening Doors, these hooks took the form of artifacts, stories, or the physical environment itself.[43] For example, a visitor to Conner Prairie might be encouraged to help an interpreter scythe the grass. The activity's uniqueness and the feel of the scythe in their hands would pique the visitor's curiosity and they would be more open to conversing about agriculture in the 1830s.

With funds from the Institute for Museum and Library Services,[44] a follow-up learning study was conducted (using the same techniques as the 2002 study to ensure consistency) in the summer of 2004 to determine the effect on the visitor experience due to the changes that had been made. This study focused on the Golden Eagle Inn in Prairietown, where a team concept to interpretation had been implemented.[45] A marked difference in visitor experience was observed by Ball State researchers in both the transcripts collected from visitors and from comments made by visitors and interpreters. Visitors were spending, on average, twenty more minutes in conversation with Golden Eagle interpreters in 2004 than they had in 2002.[46] Visitors to Conner Prairie now had a more dynamic, engaging, and enjoyable experience during their visit. The rewards for listening to and acting upon visitor input were substantial for both visitors and staff at Conner Prairie.

In January of 2006, Conner Prairie became an independent not-for-profit institution. Many of the changes taking place at Conner Prairie (which were focused on providing more entertaining and enriching experiences for visitors) occurred during a difficult period of uncertainty for the museum. In June 2003, Earlham College had fired the Conner Prairie Board (except for three individuals who had been appointed by Earlham) and Conner Prairie's president, John Herbst. Herbst's tenure saw increased attendance at Conner Prairie. Attendance at Conner Prairie hit new highs due to the Lenape Camp and Liberty Corner expansions (these expansions will be explained below) of 2001 (316,580 visitors) and 2002 (307,636 visitors). Typically in the year after a new exhibit opening, attendance drops dramatically. Conner Prairie saw 250,393 visitors in 2003, then saw attendance of 253,437 in 2004, a low for the decade of 246,728 visitors in 2005, followed by steadily increasing numbers of 258,254 in 2006, 284,608 in 2007, and 293,690 in 2008.[47] The upward attendance trend continued, with only a few bumps, between 2009 and 2013, as the museum opened the 1859 Balloon Voyage exhibit, 1863 Civil War Journey, and Create.Connect (an exhibit that explores science through the lens of history) in rapid succession during those years. Table 5.1 shows attendance figures at Conner Prairie, including the evening Symphony on the Prairie[48] concerts, in 1996 and then from 2001 to 2013.[49]

The learning studies described above began in earnest under Herbst's watch.[50] Also significant were new attractions (including a working farm set in 1886 and a recreated Lenape Indian Camp set in 1816) that were built during his tenure and drove attendance during the first years that they were open.[51] Though these new attractions did not sustain attendance, the goal for their creation was to entertain and to educate the public based on the original model for Prairietown. Related goals were to help visitors make connections between the different time periods represented (1816, 1836, and 1886) and to show change over time.

When Earlham took control, plans for further development were put on hold.[52] Earlham fired Herbst and the Conner Prairie Board ostensibly because they were overspending. Later litigation brought to light Earlham's conflict of interest in the property and an unequal division of the endowment Lilly granted to Earlham for the continuance of Conner Prairie. The remaining Conner Prairie staff (particularly in the programs division) realized that Conner Prairie should not remain static through this time of uncertainty. Changes to how interpreters were trained, a rethinking of how visitors experienced the physical space, and an inculcation of

Table 5.1.   Attendance Totals at Conner Prairie, 1996 and 2001–2013

Year	Attendance Totals
1996	272,303
2001	316,580
2002	307,636
2003	250,393
2004	253,437
2005	246,728
2006	258,254
2007	284,608
2008	293,690
2009	297,746
2010	327,829
2011	337,752
2012	328,911
2013	331,916
Percentage change (1996–2013)	21.8

Source: Conner Prairie Annual Reports, 2001–2013. www.connerprairie.org and "Outdoor History Museum Forum Report, 1996 and 2001–2009."

a new guest-centric culture at the museum continued through the nearly three years of scanty financial support and absentee management.[53]

In January 2006, with a new board[54] and a new president and CEO (Ellen Rosenthal, who had been Conner Prairie's vice president of operations under John Herbst), Conner Prairie set out to create a new strategic plan. The philosophical underpinnings of this new strategic plan were found in the new mission statement: "Conner Prairie will inspire curiosity about America's past through providing engaging and unique experiences." At the time, plans for future exhibits at Conner Prairie were guided by this entertainment-focused mission statement. Attendance data since these changes took place reflects the efficacy of this approach. Starting in 2007, each year between 2006 and 2011 has seen at least a 5 percent increase in attendance over the previous year.[55]

But how has Conner Prairie's approach to interpretation changed since the momentum of Opening Doors ushered in a new era of interactions with the public at the museum? What follows is a brief interview between the author and Catherine Hughes, Conner Prairie's director of interpretation and evaluation, on December 14, 2015.

David Allison (hereafter referred to as DA): How does the Opening Doors approach continue to inform your staff training?

Catherine Hughes (hereafter referred to as CH): Opening Doors continues to serve as the foundation of how interpreters interact with visitors, which means finding out what the visitor might be interested in before giving a lot of information. It's dialogue and conversation rather than monologue. But I think one of the ways we continue to build is to find the best ways to provoke engagement so that visitors can easily jump right into a conversation. We use the term "making the offer," from Jeff Wirth's book *Interactive Acting* (1994). We endow the visitor with the ability to respond. We also focus on how to engage in substantive conversations through the lens of history about things that people care about today, like gender equity, race relations, and socioeconomics.

DA: What kinds of evaluation have you done in Prairietown recently that have impacted how you present history to the public there?

CH: We collected another round of recordings this past season [April through October 2015] across all sites in Conner Prairie, sort of an Opening Doors 2.0 if you will. This time we mic'ed the interpreters. We are still transcribing, so still a long way to go to a report. We have been working with the Science Museum of Minnesota on a large-scale evaluation of a new exhibition called Create.Connect, which is an integrated history/science experience in the Welcome Center. Part of what we did was mic families, and we've been able to see what we're calling high-quality science and history conversations in those interactions with interpreters.

DA: What are some of the most common responses from the public to first-person characterizations at Conner Prairie?

CH: Common responses are as varied as are our visitors. I would not say there is one most common response, but a number of them. We know that first-person interpretation can be intimidating for some, which is why we work very hard to ease the way forward with certain techniques. We offer orientation posts at each interpretive area, which we hope allows visitors to understand what they can expect in that area and what they can do. For instance, in Civil War Journey, everyone is invited to help with the defense of Indiana, and are directed first to hear what happened there at the Nichols store. One frequent response is surprise. The surprise can be about learning something new or enjoying the interaction when someone is at first apprehensive.

DA: What do you see as the value of first-person characterization for your museum and what are the challenges?

CH: I see the value of first-person interpretation because it engages visitors' imagination, and through their interactions, elicits empathy for others' perspectives. It opens the path to learning experientially. The challenges are many. This is hard work to think on your feet all the time, be nimble and flexible with each visitor, to be brave and confident when engaging with masses of people.

NOTES

1. "Director's Corner," *Conner Prairie Peddler* 1, no. 6 (November 1974): 2.

2. "Conner Prairie Pioneer Settlement Annual Report: 1976: Message from the Director of Conner Prairie," CP Archive, 2.

3. Ibid.

4. John H. Falk and Lynn D. Dierking, *Learning from Museums: Visitor Experiences and the Making of Meaning* (Walnut Creek, CA: AltaMira Press, 1996), 213.

5. George E. Hein, *Learning in the Museum* (New York: Routledge, 1998), 22.

6. Willard Moore, Conner Prairie curator of education from 1975 to ca. 1977. Moore completed some graduate coursework in the folklore department at Indiana University and had worked in secondary education prior to becoming curator of education at Conner Prairie.

7. "Museum Education and Continuing Regional Traditions," *Conner Prairie Peddler* 4, no. 5 (September–October 1977): 3.

8. "Gestalt" therapy was described among psychologists of the 1970s as a holistic approach to studying individuals' motivations. Holistic healthcare also

gained widespread credibility during the late 1970s, and Ronsheim's use of the words "holistic" and "gestalt" was quite reflective of the thinking of the time period. See Kelly Boyer Sagert, *The 1970s* (Westport, CT: Greenwood Press, 2007), 9.

9. "Director's Corner," *Conner Prairie Peddler* 5, no. 3 (May–June 1978): 2.

10. For example, the people portraying historical composite characters cannot be anyone but their modern selves, however diligently they research the culture and mindset of the past.

11. "Director's Corner," *Conner Prairie Peddler* 5, no. 3 (May–June 1978): 2.

12. *The Newspaper* 11, no. 1 (August 3, 1983): 4.

13. *The Newspaper* 10, no. 4 (July 30, 1982): 2.

14. Hein, *Learning in the Museum*, 22.

15. *The Newspaper* 8, no. 7 (May 21, 1980): 3.

16. "New Programs Expand Museum Experience," *Conner Prairie Peddler* 10, no. 2 (June 1983): 1.

17. Ibid., 2.

18. *Chimney Smoke*, no. 3 (October 5, 1983): 2.

19. Royal E. Berglee, "Recreated Heritage Villages of the American Midwest: Report to Village Managers and Owners" (PhD dissertation, Indiana State University, 2000), 51.

20. Polly Jontz, Conner Prairie director 1982–1995. Jontz had an undergraduate degree in political science and journalism from Indiana University and had been the development director at The Children's Museum of Indianapolis prior to becoming Conner Prairie's director.

21. "Conner Prairie Visitor Study: Presentation of Findings," May 1992, conducted and compiled by Strategic Marketing and Research, Inc., CP Archive.

22. Ibid., 10.

23. Marilyn Hood, "Long Range Planning Data for Conner Prairie," ca. 1989, CPArchive, 37.

24. Ibid.

25. "Attendance Figures: Ten Year Trends," February 8, 2006, CP Archive.

26. *32nd Annual Proceedings of the Association for Living History, Farm and Agricultural Museums* (Williamsburg, VA: ALHFAM Press, September 1988), 37.

27. Stephen S. Weil, *Rethinking the Museum and Other Meditations* (Washington, D.C.: Smithsonian Institution Press, 1990), 64.

28. It is worth noting that Conner Prairie's "Follow the North Star," which debuted in 1999, is somewhat of an outlier in this discussion, since it is a scripted

and seasonal evening program and not a part of the core daily offerings at Conner Prairie.

29. The Museum Learning Collaborative began in 1997 as a project funded collaboratively by all the federal agencies that make grants to museums—IMLS, NSF, NEH, and NEA. Although MLC included researchers at museums and universities throughout the country, the principal investigators were Gaea Leinhardt and Kevin Crowley, who were on the faculty of the Learning Research and Development Center at the University of Pittsburgh.

30. Michael Frisch, *A Shared Authority: Essays on the Craft and Meaning of Oral and Public History* (Albany: State University of New York Press, 1990), 10.

31. Author interview with Jane Blankman-Hetrick, March 7, 2005.

32. The 1999 study inaugurated by Ellen Rosenthal and the findings from market research firms like Strategic Marketing and Research, Inc., in the early 1990s were the antecedents for this larger study.

33. Jane Blankman-Hetrick and Ellen Rosenthal, "Travels Across Time: Family Learning in Living History Museums," in *Learning Conversations in Museums*, ed. Gaea Leinhardt, Kevin Crowley, and Karen Knutson (Mahwah, NJ: Lawrence Erlbaum Associates, 2002), 305–29.

34. John Herbst, Conner Prairie president 1999–2004. Herbst holds a master's degree in education and had been executive director of the Historical Society of Western Pennsylvania prior to becoming president at Conner Prairie.

35. Author interview with Jane Blankman-Hetrick, March 7, 2005, in author's possession.

36. Mary Theresa Seig, "Ball State University Learning Study at Conner Prairie, 2002," transcription of visitor and interpreter interaction, CP Archive, 20.

37. John H. Falk and Lynn D. Dierking posit in *Learning from Museums* that through discourse analysis, specific learning indicators can be identified in visitor conversations (109). These indicators generally take the form of application to prior knowledge. As a visitor comes across new information, they relate that information to something that they have already experienced.

38. The action began under John Herbst, was continued by Ellen Rosenthal, and was carried out by Dan Freas, programs division director 1997–2010, and the programs division management staff.

39. The concept behind post goals arose out of the content-heavy focus of the 1980s and was driven by the idea that interpreters needed to provide "information dumps" for visitors through their presentations.

40. Ellen Rosenthal, Conner Prairie vice president of operations 1999–2015 and then interim president 2003–2005. Since 2006, Rosenthal has had the title of president and CEO of Conner Prairie. Rosenthal holds a master's degree in early American culture from the H. F. DuPont Winterthur Program and a master's

degree in management from Carnegie Mellon University. She retired at the end
of 2015.

41. Opening Doors began as an organizational initiative and became the basis
for a training DVD/CDROM resource (funded by IMLS) that debuted in 2006
titled *Opening Doors to Great Guest Experiences*.

42. Further research may contrast the type of dialogic interpretation in action
at Prairietown with the scripted, narrative-based styles that are key features of
museum theater. "Follow the North Star" is the closest example of a consistently
offered museum theater-style (often called second-person) program at Conner
Prairie. For an explication of "Follow the North Star" as impactful second-person
museum theater, see Scott Magelssen, "Making History in the Second Person:
Post-Touristic Considerations for Living Historical Interpretation," *Theatre
Journal* 58, no. 2 (May 2006): 291–312. As noted before, "Follow the North
Star," as a scripted evening program, is different enough from the daily experience offerings at Conner Prairie that its impact on the changes taking place
during the 2000s was negligible. The Science Museum of Minnesota, as re-
marked upon in chapter 4, has a long and storied history of using museum theater
successfully. Museum theater has a substantial body of scholarship and lived
practice around it—Scott Magelsson on the theory side and Tessa Bridal on the
practical and theoretical side—so suffice it to say that this book will not explore
that technique at any significant length.

43. This change in training coincided with the development of a six-week
seminar for full-time interpreters and some programs division managers. The
seminar, dubbed the Visitor Research Seminar, sought to examine the learning
study data and visitor experience in order to help staff gain a better understanding of the visitor perspective. The seminar proved fruitful. As one participant
(Vinona Christensen, written statement, October 26, 2004, in author's possession) noted at the end of the graduate course–style seminar, "I want to look at my
own interpretation and take steps to make it more conversational." Another interpreter (Edward Grogan, written statement, October 26, 2004, in author's possession) wrote, "I found the seminar to be much more interesting than I would have
imagined. Meetings often bore me, but I found each session we did was . . .
different from the preceding one. The questions asked in the assignments did
indeed stimulate thought." This seminar concept was expanded in 2007 and 2008
to other divisions across the institution in an effort to create a more guest-centric
culture at the museum.

44. Conner Prairie received an Institute for Museum and Library Services
National Leadership Grant in 2003 to conduct a learning study in conjunction
with Ball State University and use the findings from the learning study to create
and distribute a training DVD for docents and interpreters at museums around
the country. *Opening Doors to Great Guest Experiences* debuted in the fall of

2006 and the resource has been sold to over a thousand organizations around the country and the world.

45. See David B. Allison et al., "Building Staff Investment through Teams: Conner Prairie Museum's Shift to a Team Structure," *History News* 61, no. 3 (Summer 2006) for examples of how working in a team provided staff at the Golden Eagle Inn with more interpretive tools and ideas to provide richer experiences for guests.

46. Author interview with Jane Blankman-Hetrick, March 7, 2005, in author's possession.

47. Attendance data gathered from "Outdoor History Museum Forum Report, 1996 and 2001–2009," in author's possession, and Conner Prairie Annual Reports 2010–2013, www.connerprairie.org.

48. Since 1982, Conner Prairie has been the summer home for the Indianapolis Symphony Orchestra. These evening concerts attract over 100,000 people each summer.

49. "Outdoor History Museum Forum Report, 1996 and 2001–2009," and "Conner Prairie Annual Reports 2011, 2012 and 2013," online at www.connerprairie.org and in author's possession.

50. Although Herbst carried these learning studies forward, during her short tenure at Conner Prairie, Marsha Semmel (Conner Prairie director 1995–1997, who had a master's in art history and a background with funding organizations like the National Endowment for the Humanities and the National Endowment for the Arts) began the push to get funding from grant-making organizations for research that she hoped would lead to change in Prairietown.

51. John Herbst steered the creation of the 1816 Lenape Indian Camp (which features a trading post, wigwams, and other interactive examples of Native American life) as well as 1886 Liberty Corner (which was a working farm set in a rural "crossroads" with a district schoolhouse and Quaker Meeting House set in the Victorian Era).

52. Herbst and the board had plans to create a 1940s war-era farm across the White River (where Lilly's farming operation used to be) from the heart of Conner Prairie. A steel bridge had already been acquired to span the White River and transportation options were being considered at the time of the firing.

53. In 2004, Conner Prairie changed how visitors experienced the physical space in Prairietown. To create a space for visitors' physical and mental rest, two buildings were made into entirely touchable environments. No one staffs these buildings and visitors are allowed to explore the space on their own without any commentary from characters in costume.

54. The "new" board was actually primarily composed of members of the "old" board that had been dismissed (along with John Herbst) by Earlham in 2003.

55. "Conner Prairie Attendance Data," November 2010, compiled by author, in author's possession and online at www.connerprairie.org.

6

"THEY'RE TRYING TO LEARN FOR FREE!"

Playing with Living History in Pop Culture

In the previous chapters, living history was firmly placed in a historical context and explored from a case study approach. We've also considered a few more recent examples of first-person characterizations at museums around the United States.

An angle that we haven't explored yet that may provide fruitful insight for us is the outsider's perspective. Television shows and movies are able to capture the zeitgeist and cultural relevancy of many aspects of our society and can do so through the use of irony and sarcasm in a cheeky, entertaining way. The following chapter will explore four comedic forays into the world of museums and will showcase how the popular media portrays the strange world of living history. First let's kick off the topic with a story from the frontlines of actual living history.

STORY FROM THE FRONTLINES OF LIVING HISTORY

The storm from the night before had left a sheath of ice on the netting of our thirty-passenger balloon. John was in Belize lounging on a beach or traipsing through a verdant, humid jungle somewhere, and BJ was out of town for the weekend. That left only me to climb the balloon and knock the snow and ice off the top so the helium pressure stayed normal. The ascender's teeth repeatedly failed to bite into the icy climbing rope, and I clung tenuously to the side of the 105-foot-tall balloon. The phrase in my job description—"other duties as assigned"—took on new meaning for me.

I was already soaked through my Carharts, and my fingers were throbbing from sticking them between the net and the envelope to hoist myself up. When I pulled myself that last bit to the top and looked out over the gray Indiana winter, the peaceful reverie of the quiet, snow-draped landscape subsumed my physical discomfort, and I dutifully began the work of scraping the snow and ice off the top of the balloon.

As I finished off the last of the reticent ice, my gaze caught the line of trees along the levy. The levy had been built here to hold back the flood waters from the fertile bottomlands planted below the William Conner House. The broad, sweeping bank of the White River curved to create a swollen thumb shape around the brittle remains of the previous year's corn crop. I suddenly felt removed and foreign from this place. Conner Prairie was a fiction. A place created to evoke another time. The buildings were history divorced from reality.

FUTURAMA: MUSEUMS AS THE REALM OF MISINFORMATION AND POORLY TRAINED GUIDES

The *Futurama* episode "Jurassic Bark" first aired on November 17, 2002.[1] In the episode, the main character, Fry, finds himself visiting a museum of the twenty-first century in the year 3000. Fry, a lovable schlub from the twenty-first century, strolls through the museum (led by a dictatorial tour guide) with a glazed, bored look on his face, until he stumbles onto a display that is oddly familiar.

The tour guide explains that the wooden pizza paddle behind a glass case was used to discipline the delivery boy. An animatronic young pizza delivery boy (bearing eerie resemblance to Fry himself) is getting paddled by a gruff-looking man in a chef's toque. Fry then realizes that the recreated pizza parlor in the museum is the same one he used to work at when he lived in the 2000s. He objects to the tour guide's explanation by claiming that the paddle was not only used to spank his butt, but it was also used to move pizzas and to crush rats. The brusque tour guide immediately snaps back at Fry by telling him that she is a housewife and a volunteer who has had a forty-five minute orientation and has read Harlequin romance novels about archaeologists. Fry is incredulous and tells the guide to stop waving fancy degrees at him because he recognizes the pizza parlor and knows the place much better than she does.

Not surprisingly, the creative team behind *The Simpsons* was able to mine the self-important and often inaccurate world of history museums to maximum comedic effect in this *Futurama* episode. Not only did the minimally trained tour guide perpetuate myths about the past, she did so with an attitude of self-righteousness and irrational confidence in her stories. Sadly, too many museums have perpetuated similar situations by failing to provide adequate training for their staff—including training on empathetic listening skills—and through a lack of concern for the historical record.

Figure 6.1. In "Jurassic Bark," a 2002 episode of *Futurama*, a docent at a museum of the future describes the brutal uses for a pizza paddle at an animatronic exhibit.

THE SIMPSONS: MUSEUMS AS HOMES FOR VIOLENT CAPITALISTS

Another similar example comes from *The Simpsons* in an episode titled "The PTA Disbands," first aired on April 16, 1995.[2] In this episode, Principal Skinner tries to save money for the school. Instead of paying for admission for the students in Bart Simpson's class to visit the local history museum, Skinner has the children sneak into the museum by climbing over a fence. A soldier reenactor and his comrades spot the children climbing the fence and yell, "Hey, they're trying to learn for free!" One of the enraged reenactors then encourages his comrades to use their phony guns as clubs to pacify the children. Principal Skinner and the children look up in alarm, and Skinner tells the children to run.

Here we have biting humor at the expense of museums who are so concerned with admission prices and gate revenue that they lose sight of providing opportunities for children to learn at their venues for dis-

Figure 6.2.   In a 1995 episode of *The Simpsons*, a reenactor spots Bart trying to get into the museum for free.

counted rates or for free through scholarship programs. This vignette also gently prods at the commonly held belief that historical reenacting is populated by potentially violent misanthropes ready to cave in to the whims of a faux soldier herd mentality. The soldiers react so quickly and angrily that it is clear that a "war-like" mindset has infiltrated their sensibilities to such a degree that whacking children with fake guns is a legitimate method of enforcing the museum's admission requirements.

PARKS AND RECREATION: LIVING HISTORY AS COMPETITION

A more recent example of reenacting as fodder for humor is from *Parks and Recreation* in an episode titled "Article Two," which aired on April 18, 2013.[3] In this episode, fearless politician Leslie Knope (portrayed by Amy Poehler) finds herself at odds with Garth Blundin (portrayed by Patton Oswalt), a nerdy denizen of the fictional town of Pawnee, Indiana, over her desire to change an obscure article in the town charter. Garth demands a filibuster at a town hall meeting and after some delightfully daffy *Star Wars*/*X-Men* crossover nerd talk from Garth, Leslie takes him to task for his recalcitrance.

Garth establishes that the charter that incorporated Pawnee should be held inviolate and not changed—a position held by strict constructionists of the Constitution. He claims that the charter is not a living document and that Leslie doesn't respect the town's traditions. Leslie combats his claim by disclosing that she used to give tours of the "Pawnee Historical House" and was named "Employee of the Fortnight" thrice.

Garth shoots back that it wasn't a big deal that she dressed in costume and says that by that logic, when he goes to bed at night he becomes Wolverine—implying that he wears *X-Men* pajamas. Leslie then establishes that the people of the past weren't always the most forward-thinking folks, even though they were courageous, because they "pooped in holes in the ground" and had wooden teeth.

At this point in their argument, Leslie challenges Garth to a wager. If Garth can last longer living in the 1800s at the historic house than she can, then Leslie will revoke her bill to amend the town charter. If Leslie lasts longer, then Garth will have to discontinue his protest.

The next scenes feature Garth and Leslie dressed in late 1800s historic costume and partaking in various stereotypical living history activities like churning butter, planting crops, and playing with a hoop and stick. Neither Garth nor Leslie can handle being away from modern technology for long (especially their cell phones) and they don't particularly care for the chores and discomfort of the historic times, so ultimately they broker a deal to keep the town charter intact, but to alter the wording to better fit contemporary life.

At the outset of the episode, both Garth and Leslie acknowledge how hard it was to live in pioneer times, yet they also feel that they could have done it themselves while simultaneously doubting that the other one could handle it for as long as they could. The mindset that going back in time through historical "play-acting" is a way to understand how people actually lived comes through clearly throughout their exchange.

Interestingly, Garth and Leslie do not debate the historical record through the latest scholarship on the lives of pioneers in Indiana as a way to prove their point. Instead, both are drawn to the tangible (and certainly more risible) idea that the best way to show their mettle is by taking on a

Figure 6.3. A 2013 episode of *Parks and Recreation* features Leslie Knope (played by Amy Poehler) trying to make it in the 1800s. A dubious Tom Haverford (played by Aziz Ansari) observes the scene.

role in the past through costumed historical empathy, thus shucking aside the trappings of their twenty-first-century existence.

SOUTH PARK: LIVING HISTORY AS BLIND TO THE REAL WORLD

Perhaps the most damning indictment of living history came at the creative hands of Matt Stone and Trey Parker in an episode of *South Park* titled "Super Fun Time," which aired on April 23, 2008.[4]

Unlike the previous popular culture examples, the entire episode takes place at a pioneer village and the situational humor is derived solely from the persistence of the historical reenactors in maintaining their roles and the illusion of 1864, despite an obvious real-time situation involving armed robbers taking hostages at the museum. As the episode begins, Cartman, Stan, Kyle, and the rest of the South Park crew find themselves on a field trip to Pioneer Village. Their teacher, Mr. Garrison, welcomes them to Pioneer Village, which he describes as a recreation of the early Colorado days.

A bearded man dressed like a late 1800s American cowboy approaches the children and welcomes them to the village. In an over-the-top "g"-dropping accent, Pioneer Paul remarks on the strange-looking clothes the kids are wearing and the "fancy yellow horse carriage" parked near the entrance to the village.

Stan and Kyle roll their eyes in frustration and bemoan the horrendous nature of what they are sure will take place during their field trip. Pioneer Paul tells the kids that the townfolk are ready to answer any questions they have up in the village. The children then pair up and Mr. Garrison sends them off for their experience by asking them to "learn stuff" as they visit the charming villagers.

Stan and Wendy enter the blacksmith shop and the smith greets them and asks them if they are settlers or just trappers who are on their way through the town. Stan objects to the façade the blacksmith is foisting upon them and asks him to stop role playing. He tells the enactor that he would normally play along, but he doesn't want to look like a dork in front of Wendy. Pioneer Paul sticks his head into the shop and remarks to the blacksmith that the children are strange because he has never seen fancy hats like the ones that they are wearing.

A few notable exchanges here that showcase a clear mockery of the self-seriousness of living history museums include the obtuse way that Pioneer Paul draws attention to the modern trappings of the visitor's life (the yellow school bus that he refers to as a yellow horse carriage) and their modern "strange" clothes. While this technique is fairly common in actual living history museums, most informal education theorists would posit that it is an ineffective way to promote learning. Instead of drawing attention to the interesting historical lifeways of the past or getting the children engaged in a fun activity that puts them on equal footing with him in the past, Pioneer Paul begins the kids' experience by making them feel cognitive dissonance. They know that they came in a bus and they know that they live in the year 2008. When Pioneer Paul draws attention to this difference, he only succeeds in making the children feel like they are playing a part in a drama that they never wanted to be a part of in the first place.

Figure 6.4.   A blacksmith in the Pioneer Village regales the children as they are on a field trip in a 2008 episode of *South Park*.

Next, the children find themselves in the general store. Wendy mentions to Stan that "they had beef jerky back then" and the clerk immediately chides her by saying, "What do you mean, 'back then'?" and reminding them that the year is 1864. Kyle objects sarcastically by rejoining with the statement that it actually isn't 1864. Pioneer Paul then tells the children that of course it is 1864, all they have to do is look around them to see proof.

At that moment, sirens wail in the distance. Stan points out that sirens are blaring while Pioneer Paul claims ignorance about sirens. The sound of screeching tires is next, and everyone heads to the windows to find out what is going on. A big SUV pulls into the village and seven people some with modern guns—pour out of it. One of them is injured. Pioneer Paul and the clerk at the general store both maintain their façade of 1864 in the face of clear signals that the modern world is all around them. Indeed, both first-person enactors persist with the illusion even when someone is actually killed.

An alarmed Stan yells at Pioneer Paul that they need to call the police because someone was shot. Pioneer Paul corrects Stan by stating that the only law in their village is Sheriff McLawdog and then he pontificates about the year 1864 being a time of growth and development in Colorado. Stan then yells to Pioneer Paul that the situation is serious and that he can't be talking about history in a time of crisis.

Pioneer Paul's irrational inability to break character despite the emergency taking place at the museum is an over-the-top example of the desire for first-person enactors to control the narrative they are in as a way to exert control over visitors to the museum. When Pioneer Paul reemphasizes his learning goal that "1864 is a time of growth and development in the Old West" as one of his colleagues lays dead on the floor, he reveals himself as a sociopath with blinders to anything but the play-acting role he has assumed as a part of his job.

The journey from Pioneer Paul's extreme disregard for reality to a well-meaning historical enactor asking a visitor who is looking for the restroom to use the nonfunctional privy behind the barn is not a long one. In fact, catering to basic visitor needs like water and toilet facilities still often takes a backseat at many historical sites to maintaining the verisimilitude of the time period and staying in character.

WHAT CAN MUSEUMS LEARN FROM POP CULTURE?

Other examples of living history and explorations of first-person charac-terizations in pop culture are the various iterations of reality TV that have incorporated dressing up in historic clothing such as *1900 House* (which was the first of its kind and aired in England in 1999), *Frontier House* (set in Montana and debuting in 2002), and *Frontier Town* (in which a group of obstreperous kids run a loosely historic village in a *Lord of the Flies*–style elimination contest). These shows are all a riff on the chal-lenge that Leslie and Garth undertook in the *Parks and Recreation* epi-sode—that is, they feature modern people trying to "make it" using his-torical tools and techniques in a "historic" setting for a period of weeks or months under the watchful eye of a camera crew and then, after copious editing, the viewing public. [5]

Abraham Lincoln: Vampire Hunter graced movie theaters across the country in the summer of 2012. The juxtaposition of historical situations with monsters is alluring and has been the realm of schlocky fiction for quite a few years now. *Pride and Prejudice and Zombies* and *Jane Slayer* predated that movie and consist of fun romps through well-trod fictional landscapes (with only the vaguest whiffs of historical accuracy). The difference with *Abraham Lincoln: Vampire Hunter* is that Lincoln was a real person, whereas Jane Austen's characters are entirely fictional.

Of all of our presidents, Lincoln is clearly the most iconic. In my experience in museums, upon asking children who the first president was, about half the time Abraham Lincoln is the answer. Besides playing a key role throughout the most pivotal years in America's history, Lincoln had an exceedingly memorable physical appearance. He was a lanky dude with a tall hat and a classic little strap of a beard, whose presidency was forged in the crucible of the most significant moments of U.S. history.

George Washington is number two on the "most well-known and high-ranked presidents" lists. [6] But the 1700s were so long ago, and Washington seems somehow more staid and dignified than the somewhat clownish and jovial Lincoln. Despite old George's dapper appearance and noble mien, Lincoln will likely win the presidential popularity contest nine times out of ten. Therefore, *George Washington: Chupacabra Slayer* isn't in theaters. [7]

I am generally uncomfortable with enactment programs that put words into the mouths of actual historical people. Even if an Amelia Earhart impersonator researched the time period meticulously and could plumb the depths of Earhart's life history, it seems presumptuous and a betrayal of the person she was as an actual woman in a specific context to add to her narrative through the extemporaneous words of a modern person wearing a costume. I am not willing to discount "real-person" characterizations in museums out of hand, though. Although most living history museums and enactor programs create composite characters for their interpreters to portray, some museums (including the Minnesota History Center and Colonial Williamsburg) have been both respectful of the historical figures they portray, as well as effective in connecting with audiences using that technique.

So the blatant twisting of historical truth and the disrespectful portrayal of Lincoln in *Abraham Lincoln: Vampire Hunter* should really chafe my uppity historian heart, right? Actually, it doesn't. The difference for me is the medium and the goal. *Abraham Lincoln: Vampire Hunter* is only meant to be entertainment. Movies are the ultimate in fakery and magic, and although they often give us glimpses of truth and beauty, they are fully artifice and creative editing. Museums purport to help educate and enlighten the public. The standards for good history should be much higher for institutions that hold the public's trust.

Museums must listen to the truth underlying the humor in these popular depictions of history and first-person characterizations as they work to achieve relevance in a postmodern, easily distracted world. Living history museums that seek to enforce their fictions over the hard realities of the present may find themselves further estranged from the audience they so desperately need.

NOTES

1. *Futurama*, "Jurassic Bark," Season 4, Episode 7, first aired November 17, 2002. Matt Groening, Executive Producer.

2. *The Simpsons*, "The PTA Disbands," Season 6, Episode 21, first aired April 6, 1995. Matt Groening, Executive Producer.

3. *Parks and Recreation*, "Article Two," Season 5, Episode 19, first aired April 18, 2013. Michael Schur, Executive Producer.

4. *South Park*, "Super Fun Time," Season 12, Episode 7, first aired April 23, 2008. Trey Parker and Matt Stone, Executive Producers.

5. Reality TV received perhaps its biggest critique in the 1998 feature film *The Truman Show*, starring Jim Carrey. Throughout the film the line between reality and TV is embodied by Jim Carrey's character, who has lived his entire life on a TV set and whose only interactions have been with actors hired to portray his family and friends. Another feature film that toys with the idea of reality and the juxtaposition between modern life and the past is M. Night Shyamalan's widely panned *The Village*, a 2004 film starring Sigourney Weaver and John Hurt that culminates with a disingenuous reveal that the main characters have been living in a fenced historical village commune and have been shielding their children from the realities of modern life.

6. Brandon Rottinghouse and Justin Vaughn, "New Ranking of U.S. Presidents puts Lincoln at No. 1, Obama at 18; Kennedy Judged Most Overrated," *Washington Post*, February 16, 2015, https://www.washingtonpost.com/blogs/monkey-cage/wp/2015/02/16/new-ranking-of-u-s-presidents-puts-lincoln-1-obama-18-kennedy-judged-most-over-rated/, retrieved on December 12, 2015.

7. I'm sure scads of production companies would be willing to green light *George Washington: Chupacabra Slayer* if anyone had the gumption to concoct a script based on that premise. I jest.

7

CONCLUSION

Using Living History for Stronger
Programming and Education

Living history stands at a crossroads. The heady heyday of successful living history museums—Colonial Williamsburg, Greenfield Village, Old Sturbridge Village, and Plimoth Plantation—is long gone. Where once the techniques of living history were considered the vanguard of interpretation and experience, they are now often mired in moribund futility and—with a few notable exceptions—exist on the margins of best practices in museums.

As we explored in chapter 4, the most successful living history experiences are often one interpretive modality among many at a particular museum. Even museums that had once been known primarily for living history are now diversifying their offerings. The Henry Ford Museum has a vibrant maker space that combines history and science in interesting ways. Conner Prairie has a tethered helium balloon, a tech-rich exhibit about the Civil War, and an indoor science center called Create.Connect. Even Colonial Williamsburg, the granddaddy of them all, has started to realize that it needs to expand its offerings to keep pace in the changing economic climate. The president of Colonial Williamsburg, Mitchell Reiss, wrote in the 2014 Annual Report for the Colonial Williamsburg Foundation that:

Bottom line, admissions and hotel and restaurant revenues fell short of our goals—a reality that reflected visitation trends at museums and other historical sites throughout the country. The declining emphasis on history in American schools is making all of our jobs especially difficult—and at the same time, all the more important. Simply put, we must reimagine Colonial Williamsburg in the 21st century to reach a broader audience. We need to attract more people here, to educate and entertain them even more than we already do, and to persuade them to return again and again. [1]

Reiss has identified that Colonial Williamsburg needs to reach a broader audience through reimagining the museum and being more entertaining and educational.

Museums are no longer able to attract audiences through an interpretive technique that was novel in 1970s, popular in the 1980s, and on the decline in the 1990s. Audiences have different needs and expectations now. Canny and choosy consumers require a menu of options at museums. This menu may include living history, but it should not be solely reliant on living history to draw in visitors.

In chapter 6, we found humor at the expense of living history—like most smart, competent people, museum professionals tend to take themselves and their jobs a tad too seriously. Depictions of museums in popular culture challenge us to chuckle at the absurdity of what we do and to put our work in its proper context. At their best, museums contribute to creating a more just, informed, and equitable society. They can also build community and spur action on a wide range of issues—from poverty and social justice to global climate change and human rights.

I have argued, however, that museums are most effective when they provide entertaining experiences that excite curiosity and foster learning. Motivating visitors to change their behavior or to think differently about the world is most often a happy side effect of the rich, pleasurable leisure time experiences museums offer. Learning through fun happens most often in museums that have reconciled themselves to their role as entertainment venues. Vilifying the successful techniques of theme parks only serves to estrange museums from potentially successful and lucrative revenue streams that will support the museum's mission as an educational venue far into the future. Additionally, thoughtful audience segmentation reveals that some visitors—especially school groups—have unique needs that can be addressed through a melding of entertaining experiences with a keen attention to educational outcomes and standards. [2]

Since their inception in the mid-nineteenth century, museums have lived on the uneasy knife edge between respectability through scholarly rigor and impropriety through the glitz of showmanship. Richard Flint writes, "The direction of early museums clearly suggests that, for economic reasons, many nineteenth-century museums found it necessary to submerge the scientist in the showman."[3]

As we have seen, not much has changed since the nineteenth century. Museums still teeter between the respectable and the ridiculous. Perhaps it is time for museums to rethink their role as a keeper of the public trust. What if museums sought not merely to preserve and to educate but also to delight and inspire? What if museums could become trusted community partners and vibrant purveyors of fun experiences that our neighbors seek out as leisure time destinations?

Museums are not monolithic. Some feature highly immersive settings to transport you to other places. Some showcase cutting-edge technology to excite your curiosity. Some use spectacle and showmanship to wow you. For the most part, however, these experiential components are mere echoes of the original (and generally better) amusement park and movie theater techniques. From city to city in the United States, most museums are remarkably—and depressingly—similar.

The methods to bust out of this uniform blandness will be specific to the content, community, and mission of each individual museum. There is no silver bullet for success. Museums that have distinguished themselves, however, find inspiration anywhere and listen to their audience everywhere, all the time.

Museums are trusted, and with that trust comes great power. It is time to start using that power to chart a new course for museums. The choppy waters of the future can only be navigated with our audience at the tiller and a cargo hold full of entertaining techniques below deck. Living history can still be vital to museums as one of those techniques. The horizon is hazy and the journey will be arduous. Museums must use all of their resources—including living history—to rise to the challenges of tomorrow.

NOTES

1. Mitchell Reiss, "Colonial Williamsburg Foundation 2014 President's Report," http://www.history.org/Foundation/Annualrpt14/index.cfm, retrieved on October 16, 2015.

2. John H. Falk and Lynn D. Dierking, *The Museum Experience Revisited*, second edition (Walnut Creek, CA: Left Coast Press, 2012).

3. Richard W. Flint, "Promoting Peerless Prodigies 'To the Curious,'" in *The Amazing American Circus Poster* (Cincinnati, OH: Cincinnati Art Museum, 2011).

APPENDIX

Poems on Memory and the Past

My Brain's Acropolis

Rough, cold stone in the ancient columns of my mind,
Pitted and crumbling as pigeons beat their dirty wings in cacophonous frenzy,
Pushing like Sampson, futile until the rubble of memory piles around.

Homework Break

Numbers in straight lines, flipping through paper until tired eyes blur,
Now poolside, bronzed flesh and greasy lotion glistening with diffuse light,
Breaking through cold glassy water—sense trumps thought in spades.

Images of Yesterday

Filtered sun through translucent, bright green leaves,
Drenched in who I was, never again that place, that person,
Motes in the air, fleeting thoughts dispersed into the ether of the past.

Mortal Coil

Shakespeare used "mortal coil" in *Hamlet* to refer to a disturbance that makes life more difficult.

The modern definition of coil enriches the Bard's musings.

Coils can bounce. They are thin strands wrapped tightly, ready to be used to tie up a boat or help to close a screen door. Utilitarian. Doing what it takes to get the job done.

Beating the drum until our days here end. Hearts pumping, sending blood and oxygen through our bodies. Momentary choices set a trajectory for our lives from whence we cannot return. All we can do is continue to make choices and continue to love. We have no other choice.

But we're more than that, aren't we? A soul. A mind that remembers some things, but not others. A longing for eternity, set in our hearts before time began.

BIBLIOGRAPHY

ARCHIVES

Conner Prairie Archive, Fishers, IN.
Conner Prairie Museum Administrative Files.
Earlham College Archive, Richmond, IN.

KEY PERIODICALS

Conner Prairie Peddler. 1974–1995, Conner Prairie member magazine. Conner Prairie
   Archive, Fishers, IN.
The Newspaper and *Chimney Smoke*. 1973–1995, Conner Prairie newsletters. Conner Prairie
   Archive, Fishers, IN.

KEY PRIMARY SOURCES

"A History of the Village at Conner Prairie." Ca. 1984. Conner Prairie Archive, Fishers, IN.
"Attendance Figures: Ten Year Trends." February 8, 2006. Conner Prairie Archive, Fishers,
   IN.
Blankman-Hetrick, Jane. Interview by author, March 7, 2005. In author's possession, Fishers,
   IN.
Bolling, Landrum, to Guy Jones, May 23, 1969. Conner Prairie Archive, Fishers, IN.
Bolling, Landrum, to Eli Lilly, July 15, 1967. Conner Prairie Archive, Fishers, IN.
Bubenzer, Tillman, to Eli Lilly, January 14, 1963. Conner Prairie Archive, Fishers, IN.
"Conner Prairie Advisory Committee Meeting Minutes." September 4, 1968. Conner Prairie
   Archive, Fishers, IN.
"Conner Prairie Attendance Data." Compiled by author. January 2010. In author's possession,
   Fishers, IN.
"Conner Prairie's Five Year Plan to Improve Educational Experience for Visitors." August
   1998. Conner Prairie Archive, Fishers, IN.
"Conner Prairie Mission Statement." November 2005. Conner Prairie Archive, Fishers, IN.

"Conner Prairie Pioneer Settlement: Pioneer Craft Days Map." June 8–9, 1974. Conner Prairie Archive, Fishers, IN.

"Conner Prairie Visitor Study: Presentation of Findings." May 1992. Conducted and compiled by Strategic Marketing and Research, Inc., Conner Prairie Archive, Fishers, IN.

Correspondence between various Conner Prairie personnel, board members, and donors, 1969–1980. Conner Prairie Archive, Fishers, IN.

Crumrin, Timothy. "Conner Prairie Origins Lecture." Author's notes. March 22, 2006. In author's possession, Fishers, IN.

"Dedication Ceremonies [for the] Pioneer Village." March 31, 1974. Conner Prairie Archive, Fishers, IN.

"Director's Statement to Joint Meeting of the Conner Prairie Advisory Council and the Earlham Board of Trustees." April 18, 1970. Earlham College Archive, Richmond, IN.

"Earlham Board Meeting Minutes." June 30, 1969. Conner Prairie Archive, Fishers, IN.

Glassie, Henry. Interview by Timothy Crumrin, May 27, 2005. Transcript. Conner Prairie Archive, Fishers, IN.

Grogan, Edward, and Vinona Christensen. "Visitor Studies Seminar Survey." October 26, 2004. In author's possession, Fishers, IN.

Hood, Marilyn. "Long Range Planning Data for Conner Prairie." Ca. 1989. Conner Prairie Archive, Fishers, IN.

Lilly, Eli, to Landrum Bolling. October 12, 1965. Conner Prairie Archive, Fishers, IN.

Scherrer, Anton. "Our Town: Period Piece." *Indianapolis Times*, January 26, 1944, sec. 2, p. 2.

Schippers, John. "History of Village and Village Construction." November 1996. Conner Prairie Archive, Fishers, IN.

Seig, Mary Theresa. "Ball State University Learning Study at Conner Prairie." 2002. Transcript. Conner Prairie Archive, Fishers, IN.

"Status of Donations of Historic Buildings." Undated. Conner Prairie Archive, Fishers, IN.

Vourax, Myron. "The Conner Prairie Concept." 1975. Presented at the Association for Living History, Farm and Agricultural Museums' Annual Meeting. Conner Prairie Archive, Fishers, IN.

———. Interview by Timothy Crumrin, August 31, 2004. Transcript. Conner Prairie Archive, Fishers, IN.

———. "Underlying Philosophy and Tour Plan of Conner Prairie Pioneer Settlement in Accordance with Dr. Henry Glassie, Chief Consultant." March 14, 1975. Conner Prairie Archive, Fishers, IN.

SELECT SECONDARY SOURCES

Allison, David B., et al. "Building Staff Investment through Teams: Conner Prairie Museum's Shift to a Team Structure." *History News* 61, no. 3 (Summer 2006).

Amato, Joseph A. *Rethinking Home: A Case for Writing Local History*. Los Angeles: University of California Press, 2002.

Anderson, Jay. *A Living History Reader, Volume 1*. Nashville: AASLH Press, 1991.

———. *Time Machines: The World of Living History*. Nashville: AASLH Press, 1984.

Baker, James W. *Plimoth Plantation: Fifty Years of Living History*. Plymouth, MA: Plimoth Plantation Publications, 1997.

Barndt, Kerstin. "Fordist Nostalgia: History and Experience at the Henry Ford." *Rethinking History* 11, no. 3 (September 2007): 379–410.

Barthel-Bouchier, Diane. *Cultural Heritage and the Challenge of Sustainability*. Walnut Creek, CA: Left Coast Press, 2013.

Bergeron, Anne, and Beth Tuttle. *Magnetic: The Art and Science of Engagement*. Arlington, VA: American Alliance of Museums Press, 2013.

Berglee, Royal E. "Re-Created Heritage Villages of the American Midwest: Report to Village Managers and Owners." Ph.D. diss., Indiana State University, 2000.

Blankman-Hetrick, Jane, and Ellen Rosenthal. "Travels Across Time: Family Learning in Living History Museums." In *Learning Conversations in Museums*, ed. Gaea Leinhardt, Kevin Crowley, and Karen Knutson, 305–29. Mahwah, NJ: Lawrence Erlbaum Associates, 2002.

Blatti, Jo, ed. *Past Meets Present: Essays about Historic Interpretation and Public Audiences*. Washington, DC: Smithsonian Institution Press, 1987.

Bloch, Avital H., and Lauri Umansky. *Impossible to Hold: Women and Culture in the 1960s*. New York: New York University Press, 2005.

Brent, Joseph, and Phyllis K. Leffler, eds. *Public History Readings*. Malaber, FL: Robert Kreiger Publishing Co., 1992.

Bridal, Tessa. *Effective Exhibit Interpretation and Design*. Lanham, MD: AltaMira Press, 2013.

Bright, Randy. *Disneyland: Inside Story*. New York: Harry N. Abrams, Inc., Publishers, 1987.

Bruggeman, Seth. "George Washington Birthplace National Monument: Administrative History, 1930–2000." Williamsburg, VA: College of William and Mary, 2006.

———. *Here George Washington Was Born: Memory, Material Culture, and the Public History of a National Monument*. Athens: University of Georgia Press, 2008.

Bubp, Ken, and Dave Allison. "Opening Doors to Great Guest Experiences." *History News* 62, no. 2 (Spring 2007): 20–23.

Carson, Cary. "Colonial Williamsburg and the Practice of Interpretive Planning in American History Museums." *Public Historian* 20, no. 3 (1998): 11–51.

———. "The End of History Museums: What Is Plan B?" Paper delivered at conference: New Audiences for Old Houses: Building a Future with the Past, Boston University, September 28, 2007.

Cook, Robert J. *Troubled Commemoration: The American Civil War Centennial, 1961–1965*. Baton Rouge: Louisiana State University Press, 2007.

Deetz, James. "The Changing Historic House Museum: Can It Live?" *Historic Preservation* 23 (January–March 1971): 50–54.

DeVries, Tity. "Ambiguity in an Alaskan Theme Park: Presenting 'History as Commodity' and 'History as Heritage.'" *Public Historian* 29, no. 2 (Spring 2007).

Donnelly, Jessica Foy. *Interpreting Historic House Museums*. Walnut Creek, CA: AltaMira Press, 2002.

Evans, Richard J. *In Defense of History*. New York: W. W. Norton and Co., 1999.

Falk, John H., and Lynn D. Dierking. *Learning from Museums: Visitor Experiences and the Making of Meaning*. Walnut Creek, CA: AltaMira Press, 1996.

———. *The Museum Experience Revisited, 2nd ed.* Walnut Creek, CA: Left Coast Press, 2012.

Fahrenthold, David A. "Living-History Museums Struggle to Draw Attendance." *Washington Post*, December 25, 2005, sec. 2A, 1–2.

Faulkner, William. *Requiem for a Nun.* New York: Random House, 1951.

Flint, Richard W. "Promoting Peerless Prodigies 'To the Curious.'" In *The Amazing American Circus Poster*. Cincinnati: Cincinnati Art Museum, 2011.

Frisch, Michael. *A Shared Authority: Essays on the Craft and Meaning of Oral and Public History*. Albany: State University of New York Press, 1990.

Gaddis, John Lewis. *The Landscape of History: How Historians Map the Past*. Oxford: Oxford University Press, 2002.

Geertz, Clifford. *The Interpretation of Cultures*. New York: Basic Books, 1973.

Glassberg, David. *American Historical Pageantry: The Uses of Tradition in the Early Twentieth Century.* Chapel Hill: University of North Carolina Press, 1990.

———. *Sense of History: The Place of the Past in American Life*. Amherst: University of Massachusetts Press, 2001.

Greenberg, Douglas. "'History is a Luxury': Mrs. Thatcher, Mr. Disney, and (Public) History." *Reviews in American History* 26 (1998): 294–311.

Greenspan, Anders. "A Shrine to the American Faith: Americanism and the Restoration of Colonial Williamsburg, 1926–1960." Ph.D. diss., Indiana University, 1992.

Handler, Richard, and Eric Gable. *The New History in an Old Museum: Creating the Past at Colonial Williamsburg*. Durham: Duke University Press, 1997.

Hardin, Wes, ed. *An American Invention: the Story of Henry Ford Museum and Greenfield Village*. Dearborn, 1999. Self-published.

Hass, Kristin. "Behind the Magic: Fifty Years of Disneyland; Exhibit Review at the Henry Ford Museum." *Journal of American History* 93, no. 1 (June 2006): 161–63.

Heat-Moon, William Least. *Blue Highways: A Journey into America*. New York: Little, Brown and Company, 1982.

Hein, George H. *Learning in the Museum*. New York: Routledge, 1998.

Hein, George H., and Mary Alexander. *Museums: Places of Learning*. Washington, DC: American Association of Museums Education Committee, 1998.

Hobbs, Stuart D. "History, Memory and Apology. Exhibiting Antimodernism: History Memory, and the Aestheticized Past in Mid-Twentieth-Century America." *Public Historian* 23, no. 3 (Summer 2001): 39–61.

Jacob, Jeffery. *New Pioneers: the Back-to-the-Land Movement and the Search for a Sustainable Future*. University Park: Pennsylvania State University Press, 1997.

Janes, Robert R. *Museums and the Paradox of Change*. Calgary: University of Alberta Press, 1997.

Jessup, Benjamin. "Eli Lilly and Conner Prairie." M.A. thesis, Ball State University, 1987.

Johnson, Anna, Kimberly A. Huber, Nancy Cutler, Melissa Bingmann, and Tim Grove, eds. *The Museum Educator's Manual: Educator's Share Successful Techniques*. Lanham, MD: AltaMira Press, 2009.

Kahn, E. J., *All in a Century: The First 100 Years of Eli Lilly and Company*. Cornwall, CT, 1975. Self-published.

Kopper, Phillip. *Colonial Williamsburg*. New York: Harry Abrams, 1986.

Kornblith, Gary, and Carol Lasser. "More than Great White Men." In *A Century of American Historiography*, ed. James M. Banner, 11–20. Boston: Bedford/St. Martins, 2010.

Kryder-Reid, Elizabeth. "Sites of Power and the Power of Sight: Vision in the California Mission Landscapes." In *Sites Unseen: Landscape and Vision*, ed. Dianne Harris and D. Fairchild Ruggles, 181–212. Pittsburgh: University of Pittsburgh Press, 2007.

Lasch, Christopher. *The Culture of Narcissism: American Life in an Age of Diminishing Expectations*. New York: W. W. Norton and Company, Inc., 1978.

Lowenthal, David. *The Past Is a Foreign Country*. Cambridge: Cambridge University Press, 1985.

———. "Pioneer Museums." In *History Museums in the United States: A Critical Assessment*, ed. Warren Leon and Roy Rosenzweig, 115–27. Chicago: University of Chicago Press, 1990.

Madison, James H. *Eli Lilly: A Life, 1885–1977*. Indianapolis: Indiana Historical Society Press, 2006.

———. *The Indiana Way: A State History*. Bloomington: Indiana University Press, 1986.

Magelssen, Scott. "Making History in the Second Person: Post-Touristic Considerations for Living Historical Interpretation." *Theatre Journal* 58, no. 2 (May 2006): 291–312.

Mandell, Patricia. "Details, Details, Details: At Plimoth Plantation, the Quest for 17th Century Authenticity Never Ends. Polyester is Out, Tree Stumps Are In, and The 'Mayflower' Has a New Coat of Paint." *Americana* 17, no. 5 (January 1988): 48–54.

McRainey, D. Lynn, and John Russick, eds. *Connecting Kids to History with Museum Exhibitions*. Walnut Creek, CA: Left Coast Press, 2010.

Megill, Allan. *Historical Knowledge, Historical Error: A Contemporary Guide to Practice*. Chicago: University of Chicago Press, 2007.

Morrison, Jim. "Give Me Liberty or Give Me a Massage." *American Way* 9, no. 3 (May 1, 2004): 5.

Mucher, Stephen. "Building a Culture of Evidence through Professional Development." *History Teacher* 40, no. 2 (February 2007): 266–73.

Murtagh, William J. *Keeping Time: the History and Theory of Preservation in America*. Pittstown, NJ: Main Street Press, 1988.

Noonan, Erica. "Learning More than History at Plimoth Plantation." *Boston Globe*, November 24, 2008, sec. 3A, 1–2.

Oliver, Ruth Norton, ed. *Museums and the Environment*. New York: Arkville Press, 1971.

Putnam, Robert D. "Bowling Alone: America's Declining Social Capital." *Journal of Democracy* 6, no. 1 (January 1995): 65–79.

Redford, Dorothy Spruill. *Somerset Homecoming: Recovering a Lost Heritage*. New York: Doubleday, 1988.

Rentzhog, Sten. *Open Air Museums: The History and Future of a Visionary Idea.* Kristianstad, Sweden: Carlssons and Jamtli Press, 2007.

Rosenzweig, Roy, and David Thelen. *The Presence of the Past: Popular Uses of History in American Life.* New York: Columbia University Press, 1998.

Roth, Stacy. *Past into Present: Effective Techniques for First-Person Historical Interpretation.* Chapel Hill: University of North Carolina Press, 1998.

Sagert, Kelly Boyer. *The 1970s*. Westport, CT: Greenwood Press, 2007.

Sale, Kirkpatrick. *The Green Revolution: The Environmental Movement 1962–1992*. New York: Hill and Wang, 1993.

Seig, Mary Theresa, and Ken Bubp. "The Culture of Empowerment: Driving and Sustaining Change at Conner Prairie." *Curator* 51, no. 2 (April 2008): 203–20.

Simon, Nina. *The Participatory Museum*. Santa Cruz: Museum 2.0, 2010.

Scarpino, Philip V. "The Creation of Place over Time: Interpreting Environmental Themes in Exhibit Format." In *Public History and the Environment*, ed. Martin V. Melosi and Philip V. Scarpino, 139–53. Malabar, FL: Krieger, 2004.

Schlereth, Thomas. "It Wasn't That Simple." *Museum News* 56 (January–February 1978): 36–41.

Schulman, Bruce J. *The Seventies: The Great Shift in American Culture, Society and Politics.* New York: Free Press, 2001.

Stearns, Peter. "The New Social History: An Overview." In *Ordinary People and Everyday Life: Perspectives on the New Social History*, ed. James B. Gardner and George Rollie Adams, 3–21. Nashville: The American Association for State and Local History, 1983.

Steinson, Barbara J. "Rural Life in Indiana, 1800–1950" *Indiana Magazine of History* 90 (September 1994): 203–50.

Stone-Gordon, Tammy. *Private History in Public: Exhibition and the Settings of Everyday Life*. Lanham, MD: AltaMira Press, 2010.

Stover, Kate F. "Interpretation of Historical Conflict in Museums." M.A. thesis, John F. Kennedy University, 1988.

Synnott, Marcia G. "Disney's America: Whose Patrimony, Whose Profits, Whose Past?" *Public Historian* 17, no. 4 (Fall 1995): 43–59.

Swigger, Jessica. "'History is Bunk': Historical Memories at Henry Ford's Greenfield Village." Ph.D. diss., University of Texas at Austin, 2008.

Thelen, David. "Memory and American History." *Journal of American History* 75 (March 1989): 1117–29.

Tilden, Freeman. *Interpreting our Heritage*. Chapel Hill: University of North Carolina Press, 1957; reprint, Chapel Hill: University of North Carolina Press, 1977.

Tyson, Amy M. "Crafting Emotional Comfort: Interpreting the Painful Past at Living History Museums in the New Economy." *Museum and Society* 6, no. 3 (November 2008): 246–61.

Upton, Dell, and John Michael Vlatch, eds. *Common Places: Readings in American Vernacular Architecture.* Atlanta: University of Georgia Press, 1986.

Vanderstel, David. "Humanizing the Past: The Revitalization of the History Museum." *Journal of American Culture* 12, no. 2 (Summer 1989): 23.

Wallace, Michael. *Mickey Mouse History and Other Essays on American Memory.* Philadelphia: Temple University Press, 1996.

———. "Mickey Mouse History: Portraying the Past at Disney World." In *History Museums in the United States: A Critical Assessment*, ed. Warren Leon and Roy Rosenzweig, 158–79. Chicago: University of Chicago Press, 1990.

Weible, Robert. "The Blind Man and His Dog: The Public and Its Historians." *Public Historian* 28, no. 4 (Autumn 2006): 8–17.

Weinberg, Carl R. "The Discomfort Zone: Reenacting Slavery at Conner Prairie." *OAH Magazine of History* 23, no. 2 (April 2009): 62–64.

Weil, Stephen E. "From Being about Something to Being for Somebody: The Ongoing Trans-
    formation of the American Museum." *Daedalus* 128, no. 3 (Summer 1999): 229–58
———. *Making Museums Matter*. Washington, DC: Smithsonian Books, 2002.
———. *Rethinking the Museum and Other Meditations*. Washington, DC: Smithsonian Institu-
    tion Press, 1990.
West, Patricia. *Domesticating History: The Political Origins of America's House Museums*.
    Washington, DC: Smithsonian Institution Press, 1999.
Wigginton, Eliot, ed. *Foxfire 2*. New York: Doubleday, 1970.
Wood, Elizabeth, and Sarah Cole. "Can You Do That in a Children's Museum?" *Museum and
    Social Issues* 2, no. 2 (Fall 2007): 193–200.

INDEX

anti-communism, 12–13, 34
Association of Living History, Farm and Agricultural Museums (ALHFAM), 13
attendance at museums, 2, 70, 73

balloon, tethered helium, 83
Barnum, P.T., 1
beards, 21
bicentennial of America, 2, 18
business models and museums, 1, 30–32, 51, 86, 96

children, education and experiences of in museums, 9, 47, 50, 66–68
Children's Museum of Indianapolis, The, 42
Colonial Williamsburg, 1, 8, 14, 29, 92, 95
Community, 3
Conner Prairie, 6, 14, 63, 95; attendance at, 75; current perspective on first-person interpretation at, 76; Opening Doors transformation at, 70; Prairietown at, 26, 35, 58, 65; training program of, 21
constructivism, 2, 28
counterculture, 13, 17, 27–28; response by Eli Lilly and Harold Cope, 27

Denver Museum of Nature and Science, 53
Disney: amusement parks, ix, 30; Walt Disney, 12

Earlham College, 32, 74
empathy: historical, 55, 88; listening, 85
entertainment in museums, 60, 96
environmentalism and museums, 31–33
evaluation of visitors, 2, 45, 56, 58, 68, 70
experiential learning, 8

Ford, Henry, 14
Futurama, 84

Glassie, Henry, 14, 33, 58

hands-on engagement, 68, 71
Hazelious, Artur. *See* Scandinavian outdoor museums
Heinz History Center, 70
Henry Ford Museum, The, 2, 11, 95
human agency, 8

interpretation. *See* entertainment in museums; hands-on engagement

Jersey cattle, 5

learning theory, 9, 65–67
Lilly, Eli, 16, 25, 32, 35
Lincoln, Abraham, 92

maker movement, 3
Minnesota History Center, 49, 93
museum theater, 41

myths, pioneer museums as unique American, 7

Parks and Recreation, 87
Plimoth Plantation, 1, 8, 37
program development, 46

Rockefeller, John D., 14
Rosenthal, Ellen, 70

Scandinavian outdoor museums, 14
Science Museum of Minnesota, 57
Simpsons, The, 86

South Park, 89
stories and storytelling at museums, 48, 56

training in museums, 85

Vourax, Myron, 65

Washington, George, 1; birthplace museum of, 12–13; popularity in culture for, 92

ABOUT THE AUTHOR

David Allison is the manager of onsite programs at the Denver Museum of Nature and Science. He helps to create and sustain high-quality shows and facilitate experiences for visitors of all ages. His most recent projects at the museum include writing and developing a multimodal show on the science of flight and working on the creative team for the interactive shows and operations for the *Discovery Zone*, the museum's newest permanent exhibit.

He began his career in museums as a front-line facilitator at Conner Prairie Interactive History Park in central Indiana in 2002, and he held management positions of increasing responsibility at that museum from 2004 to 2010. His projects at Conner Prairie included co-producing the award-winning *Opening Doors to Great Guest Experiences* DVD/CD-ROM training resource, developing a history-themed play and learning gallery for children ages two through eight called *Discovery Station*, creating an early childhood outdoor experience called the *River Crossing Play Area*, and managing the *1859 Balloon Voyage* exhibit.

In 2008, he won the Indiana Governor's Award for Tomorrow's Leaders for his contributions to the museum field and the central Indiana community. He is the author of numerous articles in the *History News* magazine and a chapter in *Museums at Play*. He holds a bachelor of science in education from Taylor University and a master of arts in U.S. history from Indiana University–Purdue University, Indianapolis and is pursuing an MBA from Regis University in Denver with an expected matriculation in 2016. Contact him at david.allison@dmns.org.